MW00893111

# A Clown in Cobwebs

Walt Nelson

authorHOUSE®

*AuthorHouse*™
*1663 Liberty Drive*
*Bloomington, IN 47403*
*www.authorhouse.com*
*Phone: 1 (800) 839-8640*

*Published by AuthorHouse 08/26/2019*

*ISBN: 978-1-7283-2447-0 (sc)*
*ISBN: 978-1-7283-2491-3 (hc)*
*ISBN: 978-1-7283-2492-0 (e)*

*Library of Congress Control Number: 2019912615*

# CONTENTS

## PART ONE

## PART TWO
### My Story, Now

## PART THREE
### Family

Toss them out
Like coins
Clattering
At the feet
Of the starving
Unworthy
Those smiles
You call
Your gift
To me.


Beckon me
Call for me
Bring me to court
From silent chamber
Order me
To do your bidding
Not a servant
Really
Just a
Clown in cobwebs.

*From a previously unpublished poem by Walt Nelson*

This is a work of creative nonfiction. The events depicted in this work were real, and the people were real. I changed the names because I thought that best.

I dedicate this book to my non-biological brother, Tim Crais. He believed in this project from start to finish, and he taught me the importance of putting in your 10,000 hours. Writing this book took more than that. I hope you're proud.

# PART ONE

# CHAPTER ONE

# No Place for a Marine

"No place for a marine," he chuckled, as he looked around this absurd setting. To be sure, there were plenty of other men sitting in this family room, but they couldn't possibly understand the ridiculous situation Master Sergeant Frank Nelson found himself in at this moment. Just a couple of years ago, he oversaw one of the finest platoons of Marines to test their mettle on the island of Okinawa since WWII, then oh my God he fell, and it all went straight to hell.

Two weeks later he got her letter. "I heard that you fell into an unfilled, covered hole. They say your back is broken, but there is hope you'll walk again. Our baby will be born soon. Come back to Clarksville and see us. We can all recover together." Best invitation he was going to get. Marines have no need for sergeants with broken backs. He tried to remember her face, what it was about her that made him be so careless. Maybe it wasn't her at all; maybe it was the intense heat of the summer night. Whatever it was that led them to the act, he was now about to become a father. When they went out on the double date it was Patsy who first seemed so promising, but the mist of summer twilight is often lost in a morning fog. So was Patsy. It was Linda beside whom he awoke, and it was Linda's father who sat on the front porch without speaking, rocking in a rocking chair with a large shotgun in his lap when Frank took her home. Nearly 10 months later, and Linda was pregnant and about to deliver. Frank was flat on his back and unable to deliver anything. This was conclusively proven when he watched on Armed Forces TV, as his entire platoon's names were listed as dead after trying to capture a beach in Vietnam.

"At least it's not a war," he said as the only tear he would ever shed for them trickled down his cheek.

A door opened, and a nurse walked into the room. "Mr. Nelson?"

"Yes?"

"I'm afraid there's been a difficulty."

"What's the problem?" he snapped more than asked.

"First let me say, it's a boy," she smiled briefly, "but there is a problem. He has birth defects. When the doctor can, he will be out to explain." She must be mistaken, he thought. Marines don't have defective boys. It was bad enough that when he returned stateside his first child was a girl. Now he had a crippled boy. What the hell was he supposed to do with a cripple? Teach him to beg?

Frank had known only one boy with a disability in his life. While he was growing up in Kentucky the Bryant family had two girls then a boy with some sort of muscle disorder. Every day he would see the girls walking beside their brother on the way to school, which was about a mile and a half down a rocky country road from their homes. The boy would walk on crutches and the girls stood as protective sentries on either side of him. Frank enjoyed teasing the boy and would often challenge him to a race. The boy never accepted his challenges but would start going faster and faster on his crutches. Inevitably, the boy's crutches would slip on a rock and he'd fall. Frank would then feign concern and offer to help him back to his feet. The last time this happened Frank smiled at the boy and said, "I keep forgetting you're not a normal boy." Then Frank skipped off to school, leaving the Bryant kids trembling in anger.

"You may come in now, Mr. Nelson." Another nurse stood at the door of the maternity ward and ushered him inside. Linda Nelson lay in the hospital bed with the new baby in her arms. She wasn't looking at the baby; she was watching for Frank's reaction. If the foundations of relationships were built on tangible things, then she knew their marriage was built on sugar cubes. Keep everything sweet and nice and the house would stand. Let a storm blow through and the foundation could dissolve at any minute. Her grip tightened around her baby said "I'm strong enough to hold this burden. Don't dissolve. I can carry him for us."

Frank mustered his courage and looked at his son. The boy had his face, blue eyes, and stocky build. But the baby had no feet, just legs that stretched to nowhere. His right arm ended in a rounded point with no hand and his left arm held at its end a "c"- shaped hand with only a thumb and a pinky, no other fingers at all. Deep down inside of Frank shame was born that day. It would take him a lifetime to explore the depths of this shame, but for now, it sufficed that this was not the worthy heir to a Master Sergeant. Frank once fought his whole platoon one man at a time to prove to them he was in charge. He used to joke that he could run faster, swim further, dive down deeper and come up dryer than any man around. This circus freak his wife held couldn't and wouldn't be the son of a Marine.

Frank put his hands on his sore back, turned around, and walked back out to the waiting room. The doctor crossed over to the bed to talk with Linda. "I know this is hard to hear, but I have never seen a child with this extreme type of disability. He will not make it until the end of the week. I'm ordering the nurses not to clean or feed him, and if you must name him, don't name him a name you really wanted to use. When you're ready, tell me and I'll get you and your husband together with a funeral director." As Linda began to cry, the doctor left, and the nurses disobeyed him for the first time and took the baby to clean him. Linda named the baby Walter after her father, and she prepared to lose him.

A week passed, and Walter seemed to be doing fine. The doctor released his patients without a final visit. When the Nelsons cleared the hospital, the doctor terminated the nurses who had disobeyed him. They had fed and cleaned Walter for a week just like the other babies, and the doctor was convinced they had just prolonged Frank and Linda's pain. Neither of the two women were ever nurses again.

Frank and Linda went to Linda's parents' house to pick up their first child, Beth. Linda's father, Walter Sullivan, was sitting on his front porch, in the same rocking chair in which he sat every evening. Frank mused that at least this time the shotgun wasn't in his lap. The car came to a stop: Linda got out and tried to prepare her father for what he was about to see. Walter kissed her cheek, welcomed her home and took the baby without listening to a word. Grandpa Walter Sullivan's smile was the first one Baby Walt would ever see.

## CHAPTER TWO

# The Decision

The two-time grandfather sat on his front porch early Saturday morning and noticed there wasn't a cloud in the sky. Clouds or no clouds, he knew there was a storm coming and he didn't like storms. Long ago when he and Sarah were first married, he had built a cellar in the backyard behind the house in case of a bad storm, and if he weren't a grown man, he would have spent the whole day in it that day.

He could hear the soft muffled cry of his grandson as Linda and Frank were walking him to Walter's house. The Nelsons had built a house on a half-acre willed to them by Walter's uncle. Walter got the rest of the farm and because of his proximity to Frank and Linda; he knew he would be more immersed in their lives than he wanted. When they had completed their short walk to his house he smiled and motioned them inside without a word. Sarah greeted them and began cooing over the baby, and she and Beth, who was already there, took little Walter to the kitchen to feed him. Frank and Linda began to talk in a terse tone, and Walter loudly turned the page of his newspaper and began whistling an old tune to drown them out.

About an hour later other relatives began to arrive. Ida, Walter's sister, and her husband, Richard, were the first. In the 26 years Walter and Sarah had lived in this house they had never invited Richard inside. Walter saw no reason to start today. Richard and Ida stood at the bottom of the steps leading to the porch; they said, "Good morning" to Walter, and he went right on reading his paper without a word. When Sarah brought the baby back to Linda from the kitchen, she saw Ida and Richard standing in the yard at the bottom of the steps mumbling to themselves. She opened the screen door and invited them in. She apologized for being in the other room and not hearing them approach, but she offered no apology for Walter. She knew they wouldn't accept it, and Walter would take it back. Irish American Southern dirt farmers were a stubborn people.

Several others arrived that morning, most notably Sarah's sister, Marsha. She and Ida were the co-sponsors of this family meeting. They had both asked the family to gather after visiting the hospital when word reached them that Walter II was "defective." Marsha and Ida were in constant communication with the Lord and were often perfectly willing to share His opinion on most subjects. Many cousins also appeared. Walter called them by number in the order they spoke when they gathered. He often said that if they expected him to call them by name they should get out in the world and do something that would make them memorable. None of them ever did.

Finally, when she could stall no longer, Sarah opened the door and told Walter that everyone was waiting. Walter liked that idea, but he stood and went inside anyway. The living room where everyone was gathered was small. A couch, two armchairs, a rocking chair, a small coffee table covered in plants, a black-and-white TV, and a window air conditioner were all that filled the room. Two framed works hung near the door: a picture of Jesus looking sad and to the side and a print that read, "God Bless This House." Walter crossed to the rocking chair. No one was stupid enough to sit in it. It was Walter's chair and always would be. Sarah, Linda and Frank sat on the couch. Grandmother Sarah was holding baby Walter. Beth sat on the floor at her daddy's feet, and Ida and Marsha sat in the two armchairs. All other guests sat on the floor. They were not of sufficient rank to merit a seat. Since it was a warm end-of-June day, the air conditioning unit was humming. Walter turned it off, so everyone could hear well, and so the meeting would not last long.

Before Walter had entered the room, Linda and Sarah had served everyone finger sandwiches and lemonade, and there was a large plate of homemade chocolate chip cookies on the coffee table. Walter watched the swarm of fat cousins eating more and more sandwiches, and he silently started calculating how much this meeting was costing him. As the room slowly warmed, he reached for a cookie and said, "Well, Ida and Marsha, it's your meeting and my food, so let's get started."

Marsha, who always sat just a little closer to the right hand of God, spoke while Ida chewed. "We have begun considering the newest member of this family," she stammered, "and we are concerned what it means for all of us."

Walter could feel his giant hands beginning to perspire. "I assume you are talking about Walter?" Walter was wondering what a week-old baby could have possibly done to piss off these fine ladies already. Whatever it was, he wanted to do it, too.

"We are all very aware of the sin his parents have brought into this family," Marsha carefully introduced the subject. Walter wondered how long it would take the discussion to come around to this. He thought Marsha had better pace herself, or she wouldn't leave herself time to eat the plate of cookies.

Marsha was referring to Frank and Linda and the origin of their family. Linda was pregnant with Beth after their first few dates. When Frank was shipped to Okinawa, she discovered she was pregnant and did everything she could to hide it from everyone. Linda was always a full-figured girl, so by eating for two and buying larger and larger clothes, she kept from having to face the truth, at least for nine months. Just a couple of days before her water broke, she told Walter and Sarah what had happened. Walter was so angry he spent two days on the porch, cleaning his rifles and praying that the Marine would come home soon so Walter could do what the Vietnamese would never get to do.

Beth was born in April, a beautiful, blond-haired baby girl. She was a little underweight, but family genetics dictated that she would not remain so. Linda delivered the baby in her parents' bed while Sarah helped the doctor, and Walter protected the porch. Since both parents had only had two days to get used to the idea of being grandparents, they hardly knew what to say to each other as they held Beth. They had never heard of a man walking away from a family after creating one, and Walter was determined that this no-good Marine wouldn't be the first. If Frank didn't ask for Linda's hand in marriage upon his arrival back in the States, Walter had just the right rifle to persuade him.

"We are aware of what Frank and Linda have done. What I want to know is why does that bring us together today?" Walter was beginning to perspire around the collar. When Walter sweats, others should run.

"The Bible says that the sins of the fathers will be visited upon the sons," Ida chimed in, bits of cookie flying from her mouth. "Having this child in the family is a signpost to the world that Linda and Frank bore a child in sin. His very existence is a badge of shame for this family. I, for one, will be humiliated every time we are in public, and this little crippled child comes around. We cannot let this be the way this family is remembered. This baby has got to go. Frank and Linda should give their testimony in church and repent of what they've done, and we can move on. After all, they have the sweet little girl to think of." With this, Ida leaned forward and offered Beth a cookie. Beth was always afraid of Ida, and she put her arms around her mother's legs instead. Linda picked her little girl up and put her in her lap, so no one would notice she was crying.

"What are you proposing we do, sell the boy into slavery? Bury him in the back yard? What exactly is your plan?" It didn't take a psychologist to tell that Walter was getting angry. Marsha and Ida knew this moment was coming. They had a very brief window of opportunity and they had to take it.

"We think the baby should be put up for adoption. There are a lot of good Christian families out there who would be willing to take on the burden of raising a deformed child. We could give the baby to one of them, Linda and Frank could repent and maybe God will forgive this family and let us live out our lives in peace."

Frank had had enough of this nonsense. He may have gotten the family into this mess, but he was not going to sit there and be ordered about by a foolish old woman. When he stood to walk out of the room, Walter looked at him and asked, "Running away again, Frank?" Frank took a sandwich and returned to his seat.

Walter sat and thought a long time about what the women were proposing. Not because he was considering their request, but because if it weren't clear that he carefully considered it, this meeting might be reconvened. He looked around the room at the women in their flowered dresses and hair that resembled beehives. Unlike Walter, Richard was pale, thin and balding. He wore an old tattered white shirt and navy-blue worker's pants that made him look cleaner and more polished than he really was.

When Walter stood, it was an undisputable signal that he was ready to render a decision. "There are many things in this world I do not know," Walter began, "but there are a few things I believe. One of those things is that families are formed for a purpose. That purpose isn't to judge, censure or to abandon. The reason we live as family is to support one another through good times and bad. Families offer a shoulder when another is crying and sing along when the going is good. Anyone who would want to give away a baby because it reminds us of its parents' sin is not really a member of the family at all. Anyone who would do that is the opposite of a family: an enemy. No one in my family would give away a baby to save herself some embarrassment. I feel so strongly that is true that I'm going to ask you all to leave now except for Linda, Frank and the kids. Everyone else, go. And, Ida, Marsha and Richard, since it is my grandson who has brought you so much shame, I am going to rid you of the burden. You will never be referred to as my family again. You will never as long as I am living ever be welcomed into my home again. Sarah, please show them out."

Sarah began to cry, and she and Marsha held onto each other like bad soap opera stars who have overstretched their scene. Walter had sat down in the rocker again, and he had little patience with this caterwauling. He told Sarah to show them out or go with them, either way, but do it quickly. They slowly made their way to the door, and Richard reached for a last cookie as Walter snatched the plate out of his reach. When the excommunicated members of the family left, Walter turned his attention to the Nelsons.

"I know nothing about sin. That is an issue between you and God. What I do know is that is my grandson. Nobody in this family is particularly pretty, so the fact that he is missing body parts is a detail only. Now that he is with us, he is the responsibility the Lord has given us. He is your responsibility, and I expect you two to do your best to do right by him."

9

Frank stood; he had had enough of his father-in-law's dictates for one day. He nodded affirmatively and walked the tenth of a mile back to his house. Linda, feeling uncertain what she should do, quietly followed him with the children.

Sarah was still sitting in her chair, crying. "I suspect we will cry many tears for that boy," he whispered.

A couple of weeks after this meeting, Frank Nelson's mother, Evelin, came from her home in Eastern Kentucky to see the controversial new grandson. He looked pink, pudgy and perfect to her; she assured her son. "Mom, the boy doesn't have feet or hands. Of course, he's not perfect!"

"It could be worse. He could have two heads or cancer or something like that."

"What can he do with a body like that? He can't play sports, can't hunt or fish, or really do any outdoor activity. He'll never get a job, get married or have kids. There's no use for him at all."

"Just because he won't wear a uniform and shoot 'enemies' doesn't mean he will have no use. He will find his way. Our job is to love him until he does." Frank looked away from her as she cuddled the baby.

Frank, Evelin, Linda and little Walt got into the car and traveled into town. Evelin shopped some for Walt, and then they lunched at the counter at Woolworth's. After their meal, Walt became fussy, possibly because there was too much bustling around for him to fall asleep, and he cried mercilessly all the way home. Frank especially found it quite difficult to tolerate Walt's incessant wailing. "Linda, can't you shut him up?" he asked repeatedly. Linda knew that Frank, like a geyser, would blow predictably, and she wanted to get home before that happened. Frank went from running his fingers through his hair, to gently tapping the car window with his left fist, to shouting at Linda to "do something!" She knew he had burped; he wasn't wet or soiled, he wasn't still hungry, and she couldn't get him to sleep. Walt even kept spitting out his pacifier; what else did Frank expect her to do? She knew better than to ask him that. Suddenly, Frank pulled the car off the side of the road. She asked why, but he got out too quickly to answer. He went to her side of the door and opened it. She was afraid he'd hit her, so she reacted by holding her arm over her face and head to shield herself. He didn't reach into the car for her. He snatched that damn crybaby out of the car, walked into the deepest part of the ditch and put that screaming banshee on the ground. "Now, cry your eyes out, you little shit!" He turned back to the car as Linda was getting out to get her baby. He pushed her back inside and slammed the door so loudly, even his mother was afraid to get out. Frank put the car back in gear and drove the half-mile home.

When they all got out of the car, Evelin turned and started walking toward the street. "Where the hell do you think you're going? Frank shouted. Evelin stopped and faced him.

"I'm getting my grandson, and if you try to push me like you did your wife, I'll make her a widow."

"I'm coming with you," Linda exploded, crying. Evelin never looked back for her, but she held her hand out for Linda to take. There are times women are bound by a spiritual tie too deep and complex for most men to comprehend, and this was one of those times.

"Linda, get back to this house right now, or don't come back!"

"Ignore him. You must go to your baby. What happens afterward we'll work out." Neither woman said another word until they reached Walt, who was no longer crying. He was covered with a few dozen ants, attracted by his sweet baby smell, but otherwise was visibly unharmed. Linda knelt by him and scooped him into her arms as both women cried. After the tears began to slow, Evelin offered a prayer thanking God that other than a few ant bites, Walt was unharmed. She asked for strength for Linda and protection from her son.

All three were locked out of the house until long after dark. The next day, as Evelin climbed into her car to go home, she said to Frank, "I can't be a part of this." She never returned to their home for the rest of her life.

# CHAPTER THREE

## How do we do this?

What is it that makes a person human? We know on an intellectual level that it has something to do with our consciousness. A human is human because he can feel, relate and connect. Yet, there are animals that seem to be able to do that, too. When do we go from existing to being truly human? As the Nelsons grew more accustomed to their baby, they began to wonder what exactly his role in society could be.

First, it was incumbent upon them to address more urgent matters. What should they call him? Although they named him Walter in the hospital, Frank did not want the daily reminder of his father-in-law walking around his home all day. The diminutive "Little" Walter was far too cute for a marine. It was an improvement that they wanted to call him anything at all other than "the baby." Finally, they settled on Walt. Frank could not help but wonder, if they named it, would it stay?

Next, they had to address the issue of transportation. Would a child with no feet be wheelchair bound for life? Beth was still not walking yet, and she was 14 months old when Walt was born. In just a few months it became evident that this was not going to be a sedentary, slumbering, sloth of a child. This baby was rambunctious and raring to go. He began as all children do, with learning to roll over. Then he began sitting up, and crawling. Then he started using an alternative form of movement Linda referred to as skootching. He would sit on his bottom, and using his legs and left hand, he would slide himself across the floor. This way, Linda also noted, Walt was able to see what was going on around him as he moved, while other babies like Beth propelled themselves forward without knowing what they would find when they arrived at their desired destination. Walt pulled up on furniture early, and when he began to take tentative steps, Linda was afraid he'd hurt himself. Frank encouraged Walt's walking and soon, without feet, Walt could walk about the house. Although there was a year's difference in their ages, Beth and Walt mastered walking at nearly the same time.

Frank and Linda learned through a family doctor about a program in Nashville operated by a joint venture between the Junior League and the Shriners. These groups co-sponsored a home for children to come and be observed for a while by medical professionals from Vanderbilt Hospital. They also ran doctors' offices for Vanderbilt doctors, so they could see patients with disabilities. The whole program made medical help available for children with disabilities who come from lower-income families. Frank and Linda were in no position to pay for expensive medical care, so they enrolled Walt as a patient in the program, and he was accepted.

Since Frank's return from Okinawa, he had found a job where most men and many women did in Clarksville. He began working at the Trane Heating and Air plant. He started as a modest line worker, barely earning over minimum wage. He had finished high school in rural Kentucky, and the Marine Corps was the best education he would ever get. Linda graduated from high school in Clarksville and had no other formal education. She found work at a clothing store, but she was not much of a salesperson. She carried too much weight to wear most of the clothes she sold, and the irony of her trying to help others look more beautiful was not lost on her. Eventually she became a bank teller, a job that better suited her. She could have short inconsequential conversations, be visible only from the waist up, her better half she insisted, and she handed people money all day. What was there not to like? The fact was, however, that the two of them made very little money, and if not for the generosity of the Junior League and the Shriners, Walt would have spent his life at home watching television.

The house in which they lived was a rancher with two bedrooms and a bath. Beth and Walt shared a room, and the day they moved into the house, it was already too small. The land was deeded to them by Linda's Uncle Roy Sullivan, who died when Walt was 2. Until his dying day he believed the small bumps on Walt's left hand would one day grow into fingers and Walt would grow feet as well. Roy also got messages from his wife from the grave, so no one took his ravings seriously.

Still, with house payments, groceries, a car payment, clothes, electricity and phone bills, Frank and Linda's meager paychecks were also too small for their family. Free medical care for the expensive child was a Godsend.

Walt went to the clinic for the first time when he was 2 years old. After an examination, the doctors concluded that Walt would need some reconstructive surgery on his legs and hand. His legs were curving inward and needed to be broken and straightened. His hand was not very useful because there was very little movement in the fingers. They sent the Nelsons to a brace and limb shop to have custom-made braces designed and built for his legs.

The brace and limb guys instantly became some of Walt's favorite people. They had disabilities, too, and Walt had never seen an adult with disabilities before. He had never considered his physical difference the same way his aunts did. He was too young when the family meeting occurred to be influenced by their prejudice. He thought his hands and feet were normal. He had always been this way. No adjustment was necessary.

The shop was called Snyder's Brace and Limb, and the first employee Walt met was a man named Jack. He was a skyscraper to Walt with hair wrapped like two open hands around his head, with nothing but shiny scalp on top. What Walt liked about him best was that Jack, too, was missing a foot. Every time Walt asked what happened to it, Jack would ask Walt the same question. Then he'd ask, "Did you leave it some place? Was it shot off in the war? Get it eaten off by a lion? Lose it in a card game? Or did you loan it to a friend?" These silly questions made Walt laugh, and knowing this man wasn't afraid to joke about the loss of a foot gave Walt assurance he would never have found elsewhere.

A plaster cast was applied to Walt's legs, and braces were built for them with the casts serving as molds. The leg portion of the brace was then attached to real baby shoes. Walt was slipped into them and he could walk with only a slight limp that would be his trademark throughout his life. For reasons unknown, Walt's right leg would never be as sure as his left. Snyder's also built a brace for Walt's arm lovingly referred to as the "hook." It also started as a cast on Walt's right arm. A conically shaped fiberglass sheath was made to enclose the arm. It had a pair of metal prongs on the front of it. The upper prong had a cord attached to it that ran down the side of the sheath through a strap that ran around the back over the shoulders and around the armpit of the opposite arm. Whenever tension was applied to the cord, it would pull the upper prong that was held against the lower one with a very thick rubber band, and the hook would open. When Walt relaxed the cord the rubber band would pull the prongs together again. The prongs were also bent into a "C" shape, which Walt would later believe left him looking like a cross between the robot on his favorite TV show, "Lost in Space," and Captain Hook in P *Peter Pan*, the character Walt would be for every Halloween his entire childhood. When Snyder's finished with him, Walt was ready to wobble into the world.

# CHAPTER FOUR

## The Stable

At three, Walt had still not had any of the surgery the fine doctors at Vanderbilt wanted him to have. They scheduled his first surgery for his fifth year, to give him time to recover enough to start first grade on time. It was his and his parents' duty to get him accustomed to his prosthetics, to make them "a part of him," as Jack liked to say. After Walt came home with those braces everyone seemed to feel a sense of relief at first. They could now see Walt looking a little more like ordinary people with feet. It was possible now to imagine him walking into the world and living as a man.

Frank was not so sure. Over four years had passed since he came home from the Marines, and as his stomach expanded, his muscles converted into something less sinewy and more gelatinous, and his hairline was beginning a slow retreat. He no longer saw himself as a rock-hard Marine. That was good news for Walt because Frank could now measure him as a son, instead of a fighting machine. Even with the military standard removed, Frank still considered Walt a disappointment.

One night, after a family meal at the Sullivan house, everyone gathered in the living room, the same room that hosted the family meeting three years earlier. Everyone was seated and fighting the drowsy after-effects of Sarah's cooking. Frank watched as his father-in-law played with his son. Walter had Walt's plastic toy brontosaurus and was switching it from hand to hand and holding it teasingly over Walt's head. Although Frank didn't know the word metaphor, he knew this was an image that would forever sum up his son's life. All things to which he'd aspire would be just playfully out of his reach. Frank was not sure at whom this made him mad, but mad he was. For reasons he would never be able to articulate, looking at his son made Frank extraordinarily angry. There was something about the playful relationship between Walter and Walt that also made Frank mad. Frank had tried playing with his son, but he always frightened Walt. Walt often fell or dropped something, which would prolong any activity in which they were engaged. It took twice as long to play something with Walt as it did a normal kid, and Frank had no patience with the delay. Sarah and Linda began to discuss Walt's future, a topic that made Frank uneasy.

"There may be private schools for boys like him," Sarah offered, trying to be hopeful.

"Even if there are, we could never afford one," Linda responded.

"There's no point picking out schools yet," Frank barked. "We don't even know if he can learn anything."

"Well of course he can," Walter offered. "He learns to play games quickly enough, and he laughs a lot. It seems to me his mind is working."

"Anyone could play grab the dinosaur with you, Walter. That is no proof he is capable of handling himself in the world." Frank's face began to redden.

"I doubt you had painted the Sistine Chapel by three either," Walter retorted, unwilling to allow his son-in-law to dismiss his grandson too quickly.

Frank understood argument in this house was futile. Walter was accustomed to his role as King of the Family and would not concede a point to Mr. Made-a-Baby-out-of-Wedlock. This whole evening had been bad for his blood pressure, and he was ready to leave. When Frank was in Walter's house, he was always ready to leave.

Frank stood and said, "Well, Linda, it's time to get home and get the kids to sleep."

As he began to walk toward the door, Walter added, "I didn't mean to send you home upset. I just want to make sure we don't settle for a lesser future for Walt than he deserves. If he needs a special school, we should try to find him one. I know money doesn't grow on trees, but if we work together, we can find a way to get him what he needs."

"I want to make sure you understand that whatever Walt needs, he'll get if I decide he'll get it. He is my son, and I'll make the decisions that need to be made." With that, Frank walked over to where Walt was sitting on the floor at Walter's feet, and he picked up the toddler and walked out of the house. As soon as Frank lifted him, Walt began to do what he always did when Frank picked him up; he began to cry. Frank thought that if he dropkicked the little bastard like a football across the yard he'd finally stop crying. "Linda, let's get home!" he shouted as he put the little screamer in the car. Linda and Beth hurriedly got into the car, and Frank spun gravel as he pulled out of the driveway.

It was only one-tenth of a mile from the Sullivan home to the Nelson house, but the Nelsons drove the short distance instead of walking it whenever a big meal was involved. Even though it was a short ride, it was made more unpleasant by Walt's incessant screaming. Maybe he cried because his father took him away from playing with his grandfather. Maybe Walt could sense his father's anger and that frightened him. Maybe Frank hurt the baby when he scooped him from off the floor. Whatever the reason, Walt screamed the whole short trip, and Frank had had enough. It seemed to him every time they left the Sullivans' home or anyone else's for that matter, Walt always cried. Frank had tried spanking many times; sometimes hitting so hard the pure pleasure of it took Frank to another place. It never worked. Tonight was the night Frank decided that the crying would come to an end.

When the car came to a stop, Frank turned to Linda and Beth and said, "Get in the house." Linda told him she would get Walt, and Frank shouted, "Just once, do as I say!" She and Beth slowly walked to the house, tears running down their cheeks. Frank was pacing like a caged panther, back and forth, trying to decide what to do with the banshee in the back seat. Frank knew that hitting him or hurting him in any way would only prolong the crying, and it was his goal to get away from it as quickly as possible. Frank looked across the yard at the old stable that stood on the

19

northeastern end of the property. It was a relic of a bygone era, when the men of Linda's family were "dirt" farmers, a term to indicate what they were able to grow on this farm of red-clay soil located on a steep hillside. The stable had been a place to keep cattle when they were having calves, or it was a holding pen for cows being taken to market. Frank smiled to himself when he thought that from now on, the stable would be called the nursery. He opened the back door of the car and took Walt from the back seat. There were few child-restraint laws in those days, so Walt wasn't seated. He was standing in his seat with his arms extended up and open, ready for his father to receive him. Walt's crying died to a whimper as his father took him in the opposite direction from the house. There was no front door to the stable, just a large, gaping, dark mouth of an opening with a rectangular floor space that stretched to an identical opening in the back. With this design, farmers could drive their trucks or tractors into the building to leave their livestock or to hang tobacco on the rafters above. On each side, there were three stalls with doors that were locked closed with a wooden latch that could easily be dropped into place or opened by an adult. Unfortunately for Walt, the latch was too high for a child to open.

Frank took Walt to the last stall on the left side of the stable. He had kept Shadow's puppies in there ever since Shadow was run over by a car so he could care for them and hopefully make them talented hunting dogs like their late mother. They were blue tick hounds, and soon there wouldn't be a safe raccoon or squirrel in the area. The puppies were kept in the stall, so they could easily be bottle fed, and so they would learn this was home and they'd return here after a hunt. Tragically, caging people created quite the opposite effect.

Frank knew the position of the stall would give Walt a clear view of Frank's walk back to the house, where he would finally get to sit in peace and quiet. Walt was silent as Frank walked across the rocky floor of the stable to the stall. When Frank opened the door, Walt tensed with frightened anticipation. Walt was afraid of the dark, a condition that would surely worsen with this experience, and he was unsure what he would encounter in the pitch-black stall entrance. He did not realize until it was too late that he would be the mystery inside the stall. Frank quickly tossed Walt in through the door and closed the latch before the child could respond. Walt could see his dad in the gaps between the planks that made the door and walls of the stalls. He could see as Frank leaned close to the door and smiled. "Cry now, you fat thing. I'm going to the house. When you learn to come home without screaming, I might come back and get you." Then Frank did the one thing that made it impossible for Walt to trust in God again for many decades to come. He turned around and walked away from him into the house. Walt shouted as loudly as he could, "No Daddy! Don't leave me! I'm sorry! I'll be good! I'm scared, Daddy!" He watched as his father walked into the house, shut the door and then did the worst thing of all. Frank turned off the outside light.

Walt was frantically banging on the door of the stall, hoping his dad was just kidding and would come back for him, soon. After a few moments, Shadow's puppies discovered their new fellow inmate, and they went to the door to play. When they began to jump on Walt, he did not know what was clawing him, slobbering and pushing him. At first, he prayed they'd go away, but he had already prayed his dad would return and that had not worked. Then he used his left hand to push them away, but the dogs saw this as an invitation to play, so they jumped on him more and more. Walt could not see a thing in this dark cell, and he was unsure what was jumping on him. Whatever it was. It hit him at an unusual angle, and Walt tumbled to his bottom. The mixture of fear and falling caused Walt to completely lose control, and by the time he hit the ground, he realized he had peed down the legs of his pants. His attacker gave him little time to feel embarrassed; he realized he was confronting puppies who began licking his tears away and seemed unconcerned his pants were wet. He began to feel less abandoned, and the stall started losing its power. The puppies settled around him as he petted them, and he understood he wasn't alone.

Then the transformation occurred. Walt finally stopped crying. From inside the house, Frank stood and turned down the volume on his television. He heard the silence outside, welcomed it and sat down to make sure it would last. Frank could hear the quick intake and outburst of air that let him know Linda was whimpering again in the bedroom. If this stopped the brat from sobbing every time they left some place, Frank knew her discomfort would be temporary. He leaned back in his chair and as his eyes felt heavy, he treated himself to the luxury of a brief nap.

After a few more minutes, the volume of Linda's crying started to get as annoying as Walt's had been, so Frank stood and walked from the house to retrieve the boy. He took a flashlight with him because he didn't want to turn on the outside light and let Walt know his rescue was imminent. Frank, the avid hunter, had no problem finding the stall in the dark. He quickly opened the door, turned on the flashlight and aimed its beam into the doorway and saw his 3-year-old standing there, covered in urine, with puppies jumping all around him. "Jesus." Frank whispered, although he believed to do so was blasphemy. Walt said nothing at all. Walt saw the pee stains in the glow of his father's flashlight, but he said nothing at all. He was embarrassed by his soiled pants, but there was no way he'd cry about it now. Frank lifted him out of the stall, and the two of them walked together into the house, somehow unified by their shame.

Linda stood at the window of her room through the entire ordeal, never moving, never speaking. Her father was standing on the eastern end of his porch, facing the Nelson home. He could not see what had transpired, but he could easily hear and surmise what had happened. Walter had an old pocket knife whose blade he liked to flip open and shut with his thumb when he was upset and thinking. It was producing a steady clicking now as he opened it and shut it so fast he risked amputating the thumb. Sarah walked out to stand by him several times that night, but when she asked him what he was going to do, he gave the same answer. "Nothing. I cannot come between a man and his son." Sarah reminded him that he had advocated for his grandson since the boy came home. "I know I have," he acknowledged, "but dads each have to decide how to raise and discipline their sons. I hate to hear that boy cry, but his father is trying to shape a man. As long as he is trying, I should stay out of the way."

Sarah and Walter would always be guilty spectators in the war that was their family.

# CHAPTER FIVE
## Changes

"It's just that it seems like a lot to put a child through," Linda said with that constant look of worry on her face.

"I agree, but the doctors think it's the best way to handle it, and you want him ready for school, don't you?" Frank knew playing the school card would work.

Dr. Bankston entered the room hoping that the couple would have made up their minds, but based on past observation, he knew this was a futile expectation. "OK, let's review. We are going to do the surgery on the legs first; the ankles will be opened, and the bones broken and reset, so it won't continue to turn inward. After we remove the first set of casts, we will check to make sure all is healing properly and put on new casts to let the wound finish closing. If the surgery goes as planned, Walt will walk in a straight line without the side to side wobbling that throws him off balance now. Then, in a year, we will operate on his left hand. As you know, he isn't getting the maximum use of it now, because his pinky finger is stationary. We will open his hand, move the knuckle from the thumb to the pinky, then we'll see if he doesn't get more use from it. When Walt is around 9 or 10, we may have to do a second surgery on the legs if the curvature of the legs continues. What I need you to know is I wouldn't recommend these procedures if I didn't sincerely think they were necessary. Now what questions do you have?"

"When do we start?" Frank had heard enough. Dr. Bankston was obviously the best at what he does, or he wouldn't be the head of his department at Vanderbilt. They picked dates on the calendar, this summer for the legs, next for the hand. Then Dr. Bankston went into the waiting-room play area, picked up little Walt and took him to his office to explain the procedures to him. Walt's parents listened with incredulity as Dr. Bankston spoke with the patience of a loving God to this small child until he understood what was going to happen to him and had agreed to the procedures. Frank noticed that Walt kept looking at him to see what Frank thought. Frank smiled and nodded his consent and was surprised his son found comfort in that.

Walt's main concerns, of course, centered around how painful the operations would be and how long it would take him to recover. Dr. Bankston asked Walt to walk from his office to the waiting room. Walt did so, swaying back and forth, nearly losing his balance once. Then Dr. Bankston walked the hallway with the steady assurance of a male model. "Would you like to walk without falling?"

"Yes," Walt asserted.

"Now, this is a dime," the doctor said, pulling the coin from his pocket. "Pick it up for me." He placed it on the floor at Walt's feet. Walt tried to pick it up but could not. Finally, he licked his palm, pressed the moist skin against the coin pressed down and then offered it to the doctor. He smiled and said, "You worked for it; you can keep it. But wouldn't you like to live in a world where you wouldn't have to lick your palm every time you pick something up? Imagine if we all did that. We'd be covered up in cooties by now."

Walt's smile told the doctor he had clearance to continue.

As Frank and Linda walked their son to the car, Frank was smiling. "You know what?" he directed his question to Linda. "Our son just got a Vandy doctor to give HIM some money. He might just make it, yet." Linda was grateful for those few moments of levity.

24

Walt was too young to remember too much about the surgery on his legs. For whatever reason, it was the day before going to the hospital he remembered most. It was an impossibly sunny day. Summer in Clarksville often was filled with a haziness that trapped the heat and humidity and pressed them both down on you, making it hard to breathe or think. Although it was June, the sky looked like spring. It was baby blue, innocent and joyous without bad intent. It was the kind of day that makes people feel like running, preferably toward each other.

With each step Walt took, he kept thinking, "Tomorrow I won't be able to do this." He believed this thought might make him sadder, but instead, it made him celebrate the joy of walking. When he almost lost his balance on a hillside, he thanked Dr. Bankston that soon balance would be less of a challenge. He could see Beth off in the distance weeding flowers with their mother. He watched as she would wrap her fingers around each blade of grass and firmly pull it until it surrendered its grip on the soil. She looked a little like she was mad at the Earth and was ripping its grass out to show her anger. "Why should you be mad?" he wondered. "Nothing of yours must be broken just so you can stand."

When he shared these thoughts with her later, before bedtime, she hugged him and said she would gladly trade places with him the next day, or loan him her feet if she could. She had never seen pain, she had only heard it screaming in a stable, and did not like the helpless feeling of listening without helping. He hugged her for her kindness, and she said with her sweet baby-talk she used only with him, "Remember, we're brudder and tooder." For the rest of her life she said this when she needed a smile from Walt. It worked.

The children's ward at a Children Hospital in Tennessee was large, chaotic and filled with crying, complaining, spoiled parents of sick children, and their kids as well. Depending on the need, there were between five and ten beds in the room, with foldout chairs next to them for a parent. Walt had never seen so many children in one place before, and they were beautifully diverse; there were black children, brown children and children from all over the U.S. When the children of the nation's poor needed medical care they didn't have enough money to buy, they found Vanderbilt with its opened doors and flooded into this stadium of a children's ward and waited for help.

The nurses were ubiquitous in this ward. No child had a sneeze without being carefully inspected. The children's personalities must have been described on the charts because the nurses seemed to know how to act around each child before he arrived. They were both playful and informative with Walt. One nurse claimed when he had recovered, he would be required to bring his straight-walking self to her church and marry her, and she chased him around the room pretending to want a kiss. Without ever saying so, she told Walt he would walk better after the surgery. This teasing and the shot of confidence were the two medicines that helped Walt the most. The nurses also would spend time explaining, step-by-step, what Walt was going to experience.

Doctors were quite scarce. This adds to their mystique and allows them to charge more. Their jobs were to perform the magic and collect their God-like adoration when they were finished. Dr. Bankston was different. He took joy in talking with his patients, and Walt was no exception. Not all the children in the ward had a handicapping condition, but Bankston oversaw those who did. If he saw any difference in treatment between the "normal" and the "disabled" he put an end to it instantly. He would often be heard saying things to the nurses like, "My children get hungry, too, ladies." He didn't really have to say those things; the nurses were going to feed them just like everybody else. He just wanted the children to know someone was looking after them.

Walt understood after the operation why the staff was so nice before – so that someday he would forgive each of them for the way he felt. When he first regained consciousness, he was allowed the breakfast he had to skip, and it was just a few minutes after he had taken the last bite of his blueberry pancakes that he gave them back again in a less enticing form. Immediately after awaking, he felt heaviness in his legs, but now he began to feel the full-on pain of bones newly broken. The nurses came quickly to clean him, and as he sat up in bed, he saw his legs in casts. Suddenly it occurred to Walt that he had agreed to this. It would not be the first time he questioned his decision-making abilities.

Walt spent a week in the hospital, with Granny Sarah always at his side. Frank and Linda had to work, but they made the 50-mile trip to Nashville and the 50-mile trip home again every night. Grandpa Walter never liked to be more than 20 miles away from home, so he and Beth held vigil for Walt on the porch while he was gone.

On the last drive home before Walt was to be brought home, Frank and Linda began as parents do, to talk about Walt's future. "I just don't know what will become of him." Frank admitted.

"You mean Walt?"

"No. Dr. Bankston." They both laughed.

"I mean, what kind of job can a boy like him have?"

"Because of his disability? Well. I don't know yet, but we have to believe that he will be OK."

"Why is that?"

Linda considered, and then added, "If we don't believe in him, who will?"

"I don't mean that every time I see him, I'll tell him I have little confidence in him, but I, deep in my heart, do wonder if he will survive."

"Any doubt in him you have he will be able to feel, don't you think? How about truly trying to accept and believe in him? Would it cost you so dearly to invest your faith in him? If you're right and he does make something of himself, then you will have the advantage of being on the right side. If you are wrong, and he is a complete failure, then the worst that can be said of you is that you loved your son."

"I'll try." Frank had never heard her argue so passionately before, and he knew he was treading on thin ice.

"You'll have to commit more than that," Linda insisted.

"I'll try." Frank whispered.

Walt came home the next day, and it was a joyous occasion for all. Even Beth got to make the trip to Nashville to get Walt, and when everyone arrived home a "Welcome Home!" banner hung from the front of the Sullivan home like a big smile.

Walt looked carefully at the house he could no longer reach on his own. It dawned on him, really for the first time, that he would be dependent on someone to take him wherever he needed to go. This was not a new thought because all children are dependent on others to go from one place to another. What made this different was Walt knew getting him in and out of a wheelchair each time he rode in a car would annoy Frank and would lessen Walt's chances of getting out of the house. Suddenly, Walt noticed the windows surrounding the banner joined with it to make a face. Was it smiling because Walt was finally home or because it knew it would hold Walt captive there? Only time would tell.

It took Walt about three months to recover from the initial surgery. Walt wasn't really reading yet, but Grandpa Walter had a friend at work who liked comic books, and Walt received a bag full of them every week. During the weekdays, Walt and Beth stayed with Sarah while the parents worked, and Sarah often got Walt to make up stories to match the pictures he saw in the comic books. She also gave Walt paper and a child-sized pencil and taught him how to draw. She had learned to draw bunny rabbits when she was a child, and although this was all she could draw, by teaching Walt this technique, it seemed to give him permission to imagine and draw much more. While he enjoyed looking at the books, making up stories, and drawing, he couldn't help but watch Beth playing in the front yard with her dolls. "What's wrong?" Sarah asked him one day when she saw him staring out a window.

"I miss going out to play," he sighed.

"You get to play, too. It's just that you play in your mind."

"Playing in the warm sun is better."

"Yes, but an active imagination will last you longer."

When the casts had completed their jobs, they were removed. To Walt's great disappointment, this did not mean he could walk. "You see, Walt, your legs have weakened since you've been in casts. You are going to have to strengthen them again," Dr. Bankston explained after the casts were removed.

Walt began slowly by practicing standing. This task was made harder by the fact that the end of his leg ended at a rounded point and all his weight was focused on one point at the end of each leg, instead of on a nicely designed arched foot. When his standing became less painful, Frank decided it was time for Walt to move on to the next task. He told Sarah that, "During the day, Walt is to stand in front of your couch and walk back and forth from one end of it to the other. It is OK for him to bend over and balance himself with his arms on the couch, but he must keep walking."

"That seems harsh and cruel," she responded.

"Not as cruel as confining him to a wheelchair for the rest of his life.

Also, when he needs something like his lunch, a drink or a comic book, put it at the opposite end of the couch and make him walk to it."

Although the words, "Yes, Sarge!" were bouncing around in her mind, she decided not to say them aloud. She did then and there decide, however, that she would be watching the boy without Frank's help; she would do this her way. She confined the time Walt had to walk up and down the couch to a couple of hours a day – one in the morning and one after his afternoon nap. The rest of the day he crawled on his knees where he had better balance and was still strengthening his legs. She also refused to make him walk to the other side of the couch for what he wanted or needed: She never begged; her grandson wouldn't either.

# CHAPTER SIX
## Changes II

**D**r. Bankston knew this would be the hardest sell of them all to Walt. How do you explain to a little boy that you are going to make him incapable of doing anything for himself for a few months, to liberate him for a lifetime? Boys his age can't tell the difference between an afternoon and the rest of their lives, so how can you make sense of this surgery? The idea of faith is born during childhood because children have no choice but to believe in the hocus-pocus adults sell them. Dr. Bankston would tell Walt that he would take a knuckle out of his thumb, put it in his pinky, and suddenly, Walt's hand would significantly increase its productivity. And Walt would buy this because Dr. Bankston wears a white coat, has a Dr. in front of his name and works in a hospital. How easily the coat could morph into a collar; the doctor a reverend; a hospital a church. Science is the new religion, but the same faith is still demanded of the followers.

Walt and his parents entered the room not aware that it was time to discuss surgery again. He was just beginning to understand how much easier walking will someday be for him. When Bankston told him what was next, he was unprepared for Walt's objection. "I just finished learning to walk again," he moaned. "What will I have to do this time?"

"You will have to be patient and let others help you." The doctor explained the procedure as simply as he could, and Walter's parents saw the wisdom in the surgery: Walt saw that it wasn't their hands that would be affected. Dr. Bankston showed Walt how his pinky wasn't movable or growing very much, and by moving Walt's fingers for him, explained the limited flexibility his fingers had without the surgery and how they would improve with it. Walt smiled and said, "I trust you Dr. Bankston. If you think this will help, then OK."

"You just agreed to change your life for the better, forever!" Bankston nearly shouted. There was a feeling of celebration in the room. Nurses came in and assured Walt that he would love his newfound freedom. Everyone started pressing his or her thumb to his or her pinky, picking up a variety objects, and passing them to others. Walt's mom was explaining to him how he could feed himself with this new change.

Walt did not take part in this impromptu party; it seemed he blinked, and he found himself in a hot, scratchy cast, separated from his sister who was playing outside, uninhibited, carefree and without pain. He was sitting in the Sullivan living room, the black-and-white TV was babbling loudly enough to drown out the end of winter, and once again he had sat out a season.

Living with Walt's only truly functional arm in a cast was extremely limiting. Walt couldn't do much for himself; he couldn't dress himself, nor could he write or draw. He could feed himself such things as sandwiches, chips and cookies, staples in any boy's diet. If he wanted anything more complicated, someone had to feed him. The job always went to Sarah or Linda. Men were too important to feed helpless children. Beth enjoyed feeding Walt, but Walt did not enjoy her sense of humor at his expense. She would give him too much and make him spill food, or too little to try to get him to beg for more. She once lined green beans up on a table and asked Walt to bend down and pick them up with his lips and eat them. He didn't; an argument ensued; Linda and Sarah became the only ones who would feed Walt.

Finally, the day arrived for the removal of the cast. A little circular saw cut through the cast. Then, the cast was torn apart and removed.

Underneath it was an arm that looked like it had been buried for a year. Dead skin brushed off the arm in leaves, and that scared Walt at first. Dr. Bankston assured him that it was normal to lose a couple layers of skin. After the larger pieces came off, Walt could still scratch it and the arm would "snow" small flakes of skin for days. Walt made it "snow" on Beth often as payback for her food torture. The purpose of the surgery was to give Walt's hand more agility, and the surgery seemed to be a success. Walt soon was feeding himself, dressing himself, and writing with a first-grade big pencil. He would be able to function next year as a first-grader, and this was a big relief to Linda and Frank.

One morning in April, Linda came into the children's room to get Walt out of bed. For the first time, he noticed that Linda had grown much larger in the last few weeks. Her belly was rounded, and she seemed to be moving slower than usual. Before she lifted him, she put her hands on her sides and stretched backward to relieve the stress that her back was about to face. She lifted Walt, then called for Frank. Walt wondered what he had done to hurt her. She was leaning on the bedpost when Frank entered, and he shot a glance at Walt to let him know that Walt would be punished if this was his fault. Linda said, "I think it's time. Call Momma to come get Walt and Beth. We're going to the hospital." The sergeant sprang into action and Walt knew he was off the hook.

When Sarah arrived, Frank and Linda sat the kids down to talk with them, briefly. "We have a surprise for you." Linda was giddy. "We are going to the hospital to get you a little brother."

"I already have a little brother," Beth objected. "Can't you get a girl this time?"

"We don't get a choice, Honey. We get the baby God sends us." Frank looked sadly at Walt as this explanation was offered.

As the parents walked quickly to the car, Linda leaning heavily on Frank's shoulder, Walt heard them whispering. "It's finally a boy …"

Walt's 4-year-old intellect couldn't decipher the meaning of his parents' mysterious comment, but it was to run through his mind for the rest of his life.

"It's finally a boy …"

# CHAPTER SEVEN

## Another Frank

The new baby came home just a couple of days later. His name was Frank Nelson Jr. Linda, upon arriving home, decided she needed to talk with Walt about the name. "When you were born, the doctors told us you would not live very long, and we shouldn't use whatever name we had planned to use. We should use it on a baby who had a better chance of living and not waste it …" Linda realized quickly she wouldn't be able to take back those last words.

"So, if I weren't born handicapped, I would have been named Frank?" Walt questioned.

"Yes," Linda was honest.

"I got lucky, I guess. Who wants an ugly name like Frank?" Linda and Walt walked silently into the bedroom where little Frank was sleeping and peered over the rails of the crib.

"He does look like Daddy," Walt added.

"So do you, son." Walt wasn't sure how to react to this. He had heard parents play the "looks like" game, but he had never been the topic. When he was discussed, it was always with pity. "Isn't it a shame that he …Will he ever be able to … I wonder why they …" These were the kinds of discussions that dropped around him like unwanted raindrops, making it hard to see into his future clearly. Suddenly, his new brother, brand new to the world, was already taking his place of honor at the table beside his father. They look alike; surely they will be alike. Frank Jr. will have a future and a family, and he is the culmination of all the genetic divisions and revisions that have been the vines that have decorated the walls of their fortress.

# PART TWO

# My Story, Now

# CHAPTER EIGHT

## Starting School

They say generals often remain awake all night anticipating the upcoming battle the next day. I don't know if she slept well or not that night, but the next day, my mother was about to go into a battle she knew instinctively must be fought even though she would not really understand its importance for years to come. Just like Lee found himself suddenly fighting in Gettysburg, my mom would find high ground inside the front door of an Elementary School near my neighborhood. We entered the doorway as hundreds of other mothers must have entered with their children; Mom had me by the newly restructured hand and walked with me on my newly reshaped legs up the stairs and through the front doors. Everyone was looking at us. I assumed they were astonished that anyone so young would have a new hand or legs, and I thought they might be all the rage come Christmas. Every child who encountered me would want new limbs! And why not? I could walk up stairs, down stairs, open the doorknob, dress and feed myself all in a day. Who wouldn't be envious?

It was at that moment I would meet the great enemy of our age: the school principal. Who remembers his name, or even cares? He was some struggling educator whose inabilities and lack of creativity in the classroom were rewarded with a doubling of pay and with something teachers would need more than he: an office and secretary. While thousands and thousands of teachers fight mounds of papers, swirling about them in a sea they could not surf as they also planned classes and taught children, each principal got a secretary who would type the one or two letters for him a day, answer his phone and fill out paperwork for a central office that was inevitably less relevant than the principal.

This principal looked at me for the first time with a clear lack of appreciation for the ingenuity of the medical geniuses at Vanderbilt Medical. "Special Ed is down the hall," he said pointing to his left.

"I don't believe a Special Education will be needed for my son," my mother declared. "He can already read and write. His father and I want him educated just like any other child." Special Education in 1966 was nothing more than a parking lot for children with disabilities. They would go to lunch at a different time from the other children so their appearance wouldn't disturb the others. They learned words like, "Yes, ma'am" and "No, sir" and learned to watch silently while others talked. They were also, in high school, taught marketable skills, like how to clean bathrooms and mop floors; talented and esthetically pleasing kids got to learn such phrases as, "Welcome to …" and "Have a great day!" All of them learned to fold boxes, repeatedly, all day long.

"Now, Mrs. Nelson, special ed is where we assign all children like your son." The principal smiled broadly while stereotyping me.

"By 'like' my son you mean crippled?"

"Why, yes?"

"That boy was born without hands and feet; his mind is perfectly intact. I don't want you to teach him to sit in a room all day. I want him reading, writing, doing math and learning about the presidents just like all the other kids?"

"You mean like the normal kids?"

Although she would not use it very often in her life, Linda Nelson did have a backbone, and she could feel it tingling with life now. She stood taller than she ever had before and found the courage to argue with a man. I saw her that day for the first time. I realized that if my father had ever loved anyone, she could have been a great person. Years later, he would cling to her to prevent his descent into a mental Hell, and he would talk about love, but it was only a word to stave off the inevitable. He would never love, nor would he ever see the warrior woman I saw that day, standing up for her son.

The battle between these two went on for what seemed like an eternity. Linda was strengthened by the knowledge that she was protecting her cub; the principal was fueled by the certitude with which all educators can sit in judgment of their students. The principal had often assigned students with a cavalier flip of the wrist, and if he second-guessed this one, would he have to go back and rethink his other hasty decisions?

At some point, the teacher of the class outside of which Mom and the principal were fighting opened her door and asked what the problem was. Both answered, and she looked hard at Mom. "Aren't you Linda Sullivan?" she asked.

"Used to be, Mrs. Ussery. I'm Linda Nelson, now, and this is my son, Walter. Your principal wants to place him in special ed, but I want him to get a normal education. He can already read and write."

Mrs. Ussery knelt to look me in the face. She was a woman nearing retirement age, with cat-eye glasses, a plain dress and gray hair pulled back into a bun. She asked me what I liked to read, and I answered her. She asked me to count to 50, and I did. She asked me if I were smart. I said, "I don't know." She stood up then, physically and metaphorically, and accepted me as a student in her class.

The principal shouted, "He's clearly handicapped!"

"He looks like a student to me," was her only reply to him. She took me by the hand, something rarely done, and walked me into the room. "You have to do me a favor if I'm going to teach you, Walter. When asked if you're smart, from now on, say yes. Can you do that for me?"

"Yes, ma'am."

"Call me Mrs. Nell. I think we will get along fine."

# CHAPTER NINE

# Acceptance?

On the first full day of school I had to ride with Beth on a school bus. In a nearly 45-minute drive from our house to the school, we picked up kids of all sizes and shapes. The next kid to get on after me and Beth was a boy named Dewayne. He came to the center where I was sitting and joined me without asking. "You the Nelson kid?"

"Yeah, Walt's my name." I offered my hand, but he didn't seem to notice.

"Sounds like an old man's name," he mused.

"I'm named after my granddaddy."

"Me, I'm Dewayne Jr. People say I even look like my dad."

"Good for you ..." I was not very interested in this conversation. As he continued to talk about his dad, the bus turned around at the end of our street, came back to the street past our church and stopped about a mile from it. Two girls got on the bus, sisters named Cheryl and Rosa. Rosa was my age, with a mane of hair worthy of a lion. She walked down the aisle and as she came next to our seat, she made eye contact with Dewayne, if for only a brief second. She continued a couple of seats behind us and on the opposite side of the bus and sat down. To keep from looking back at Dewayne, she took a picture from a notebook and looked at it, feigning interest. After watching her for a moment, Dewayne turned to me and suggested I go talk to her.

"She didn't even look at me," I protested, hoping to be proven wrong.

"She's just being cool. Go talk to her anyway.

I don't know why but I did. I sat on the seat in front of her, and I introduced myself. She told me her name was Rosa and she was happy to meet me. She didn't look happy, and I said so. She then showed me the picture; it was of Elvis Presley. I had no idea who that was, but he seemed a bit old for her. She didn't appreciate my delicate maneuvering to win her heart and explained that he was famous and although they had never met, he was the guy for her. I shot; I missed. In came the professional closer. Dewayne began explaining to Rosa the fascinating spiritual connections that bound him to his dad and made his name perfect, and I moved back to my original seat.

When it was time to get off the bus, Dewayne and Rosa jumped and got out faster than I. They were waiting for me as I got off the bus, and they pulled me aside away from the flow of riders dismounting the bus. Dewayne glanced back at Rosa looking for reassurance, then spun around and punched me right in the mouth. I would love to tell you that I turned huge and green, ripped Dewayne's arm off, made schools safe from bullies for all time and became the first member of the Justice League with a disability, but the truth is I spun and slowly settled to the ground like a dreidel. Rosa peered down at me with that, "To the victor go the spoils" look, and she and the "victor" walked away arm in arm while I attempted to stand and walk through the gathering crowd that offered no helping hand at all.

The first day of class was much less painful than its auspicious beginning, but every kid in the school knew I had lost my first battle and seemed to be scheming to beat me again as they whispered as I passed, and they surreptitiously made their hands look like mine. Anyone who says that imitation is the sincerest form of flattery has never been mocked.

Over the first few weeks we learned numbers, letters, colors and all the things I knew before I started school. After a few weeks, however,

Mrs. Nell began to change the rules: It wasn't good enough to know your numbers; you had to combine them or divide them in various ways. It was something called math, and it clearly wasn't for me. Mrs. Nell would start each lesson having students hold up their fingers. When she realized I only had two to contribute, she must have known the exercise would leave me feeling alienated. Yet, that was the way she had always taught it …

One day, while my peers were subtracting, Mrs. Nell had a stroke of genius. She picked up two cans wrapped in paper and used as pencil holders and placed them on my desk. Then she put five pencils in each can. She told me they would represent my hand and allow me to do the same math as the other kids. This was my first modification before educators were even using the term, and Mrs. Nell did it for the reason most teachers do – she wanted to teach me.

Recess was apparently not for me because it seemed like every day they had a new reason to keep me inside. I either didn't finish something, or I finished it too early. Sometimes I said the wrong thing and sometimes I said nothing. Whatever I decided to do never seemed to satisfy anyone, so I sat in the classroom and listened to the sound of children playing as I "worked." I am not so old that I attended a one-room schoolhouse, but my school was an old wooden structure, and each classroom had a back door that released onto the playground. The playground was a dusty pit with a merry-go-round, a seesaw, monkey bars, a swing set and slide, and a very short basketball hoop that never saw a net.

Sometimes I rode the merry-go-round, but I'd get dizzy easily and become disinterested. I never made it past the first rung of the monkey bars, never tried the seesaw, and swings were seats to seasickness. On the few days I was permitted to go to recess, I found myself with very little to do.

One day, four boys had to stay in with me during recess. We had finished our work, and Mrs. Nell was at her seat grading it. She said we could talk quietly while she graded if we wanted. The boys gathered in a huddle near my desk and began to brag about their lifetime of heroic accomplishments. They spun tall tales about baseballs being batted further than anyone could have guessed, girls kissed and bike crashes survived. As their stories began to wane, they looked sadly at me. I could see in their eyes that they were trying to excuse me from this exercise, but I didn't want to be excluded. After a few awkward seconds, I saw the answer to my problem. The room was warm as windows filled with spring sunlight, and on the window next to my desk was a sleepy wasp trying to find an acceptable way to fall asleep while vertically clinging to a pane of glass. He was slowly opening and closing his wings, and I was inspired to be cruel to be cool. Without explaining anything to the other boys, I reached out with my hook, and snagged the wasp by the closed wings. They jumped up from their seats screaming and laughing, and Mrs. Nell grumbled for us to quiet down.

If you believe the Urban Legend of this story, I used this wasp to sting my new friends, but I didn't do that. I opened the window and released the wasp into the spring air and sat before Mrs. Nell could complain. The boys told me that was the coolest thing they had ever seen, and when we were finally allowed to go outside, they rapidly spread the story around the playground. Suddenly, I wasn't just the fingerless kid who got punched in the mouth: I was Walt, the Wasp Master. I didn't know then that first grade was a series of victories and losses; soon I'd learn all of life is.

CHAPTER TEN

# Walls

With street cred comes street challenges, or so I discovered after the wasp incident. There was a boy in my class named Kevin. I am not certain about this, but I believe Kevin was already shaving in the first grade. To say he was a little intimidating to a dreidel was an understatement. When he heard I caught the wasp, he suddenly seemed to want me to die. On the rare occasion I could go to recess, he met me at the door. "I'm going to give you a beating, Nelson," he said every time I left the classroom.

I would attempt, usually successfully, to stall him. I would ask him questions he couldn't answer like, "What is the opposite of 'no'?" Or "What celestial orb orbits the Earth?" Tricky questions like that could undo a guy. While Kevin thought about the answers, I would slip away undetected to live and fight another day. One day, the game came to a climax.

"No questions today, boy. Today, you die." I couldn't help but be proud. Kevin had built a sentence and a fragment on his own all on the same day. When he grabbed my collar, I was less amused.

"Kevin," I began, holding up my hands. "Clearly I cannot fight you. I have no fists. I can't even help you tie your shoes." They did need attention, but he didn't look. He was a warrior. As I glanced around the schoolyard, I kept looking at the statue-like faces that stared back at me stoically removed from my misery yet seemingly curious about the outcome.

Looking at their faces led me next to noticing the stone wall that surrounded the school. It was gray stone cemented into a five-foot prison wall that stretched across the front lawn of the school, except for a space for an entranceway, and it enclosed both sides of the school with a play area as the barrier in the rear of the school. This wall was meant to hold us in, but I quickly realized it was my means of escape.

"I have an idea!" I looked expectantly at Kevin, hoping he wouldn't guess my ploy. "Let's go to the front wall and have a kicking contest. We'll take turns kicking the wall to see who can do it the hardest. The hardest kick wins; what do you say?"

"I know what you'll do," Kevin retorted. "You'll have me kick first, and after I have kicked hard enough to hurt myself, you'll barely tap the wall. I'll win but I'll get hurt." Good plan. Wish I had thought of it.

"No! I'll kick first, if you like." Neither Kevin nor the other kids in my school had any idea that I wore prosthetics on my legs and had no feet. They only knew about the part of my "disability" they could see. Maybe they would have known more if they had ever asked me any questions, but it was much easier to find the rumored answer to your question than to take the bold step of asking me personally, so my peers knew almost nothing about me. Kevin had issued the challenge; he could hardly back away from it. We walked to the wall in silence while a crowd gathered around us.

When we arrived at our destination, I knew it would be important to show no fear. I stepped up to the wall and after a couple of practice swings, I kicked the wall harder than humanly possible. I jumped around like a fool for a few minutes, shouting, "Owwww! Owww!!" Then I seemingly regained my composure, walked in a circle, and came to a silent stop. "Your turn. Be careful. It really hurts."

Kevin obviously was very suspicious of my performance. He didn't believe my show of pain, but he had no idea why not. He looked at me, and then he looked back at the wall. He looked at me, then the wall. Me. The wall. Me. The wall. Then, Kevin kicked the wall with all his might.

He screamed and suddenly the schoolyard filled with teachers. Kevin was taken to the hospital. He broke two toes, it turns out. I was taken to the principal's office.

"Stop smiling!" he grumbled as he came in to talk with me. We had a new principal after the first week of school. I don't know why they assigned us a new one, but Mr. Stephen Bryant seemed to like and understand kids. He asked me what led to the confrontation that had just occurred. I told him about all the times I'd been threatened. "I guess you think Kevin had this coming?"

"Yes."

Then I saw it. He began to have trouble containing his smile. "Me, too."

# CHAPTER ELEVEN

# Better Than Before

After dealing with Kevin on the schoolyard, I became the temporary king of the playground. My teacher stopped trying to keep me inside because she realized she didn't have to protect me. Word soon traveled around the school that I had artificial legs and that's how I was able to kick the wall so hard. I know this word got around because I heard kids whispering about it on the playground. No one ever actually asked me about my legs, asked me to describe them, or asked why they were artificial. People always seemed to be more comfortable with walking around me in circles, discussing me among themselves than with coming right out and asking me a question. Maybe they thought I'd break their toes if they asked? Some days I might have.

A few weeks after my first winter break, we had a day in school while freezing rain and snow slowly covered the landscape in a solid sheet of ice. If there is any obstacle in the world I cannot seem to overcome, it is ice. I am Napoleon and ice is my Russian winter. I can go no further; I must turn back and suffer my losses.

As the rumors that school would let out early began to circulate, I grew more and more worried. How would I make it to the school bus and from the bus to the house?

I asked the teacher if I could go talk with Beth. Beth came to the classroom door looking very annoyed. "What do you want?"

"I'm worried about the ice. When they dismiss school and we have to load the buses, I don't know how I'll make it."

"How is this my problem?"

"I'm your brother. Come on, say you'll help me."

"How do you want me to do that?"

"Let me lean on your shoulder until we get to the bus." It didn't seem unreasonable, and even if she didn't plan to, at least she could lie and say she would to stop me from being so worried. But she turned around without answering, and she walked back to her seat. We were released right after lunch because it would be cruel to send kids out into the world without fortifying them with cafeteria hot dogs. As my class arrived at the door, I could see the front lawn, trees, buses, cars and electric wires were all covered with a sparkling white sheet that looked like wet plastic.

Several kids were loading their buses. They were intentionally skating, laughing, throwing snowballs. They were reacting to snow the way most kids would when just given a half-day off. When I stepped through the schoolhouse doors onto the landing, it was as if a spotlight hit me and dramatic music began to play because they all stopped and watched to see what I'd do. The steps were vacuum sealed with ice. The temperature wasn't so cold that it was a cloudy, dry ice. It was clear and wet, making it ever more treacherous for me. I knew that even if I firmly held the handrail my legs would immediately slip out from under me if I attempted to descend the steps. Instead, I turned around in a circle, asking if anyone could help me. Nothing. The silence of my audience was now complete. When I made eye contact, it was directly returned. No one dared to avert his gaze and miss the opportunity to watch the legless kicker of walls fall. I had no choice. I turned my back to the schoolyard and knelt on my hand/arm and knees. I crawled backward off the steps. Right before my knee touched the final step, I slipped, slid over the step and onto the sidewalk. The sidewalk was divided into very large squares and fortunately the top one was flat, so I didn't continue bowling-ball style all the way to the bus.

I got on all fours, turned to face the bus, and seeing that the shortest route was not by sidewalk but by the lawn, I began crawling over frozen grass. I tried to imagine that I was Godzilla trampling tiny trees on my way to Tokyo, but the burning stares I kept getting reminded me that I was a cold and lonely boy being humiliated before his peers. My hand and arm were getting increasingly cold and my pants were wet and hopelessly stained. I stood on my knees to warm my hand and arm in my pockets; I kept my gaze on the ground, on the objective ahead of me. I wasn't feeling ashamed anymore. I was determined to reach the bus. Their judgment meant less and less to me as the cold purified my worries.

I finally reached the bus. I crawled up the stairs, and when I could, I stood. The bus driver caught my gaze first. He pursed his lips as if to say something to me. "Please don't," I asked of him. He stayed silent. I sat on the front seat, cleared for me by elementary students. No one said a word on the ride home that day. From time to time, students getting off the bus would look at me. I looked past them, beyond them. I didn't want to be mad at them, but I didn't want to feed their sense of victory, either.

A few days later while I was sitting in my regular spot in the bus, Dewayne joked that I looked like a dog crawling to the bus. Everyone got quiet again, awaiting my response. I said, "I was going to pee on the tires, but it was too cold." Everyone laughed. All was forgiven, but not forgotten.

As the first and second grades began to melt into memory, the doctors noticed I was having more and more difficulty walking. Dr. Bankston had me walk up and down the corridor enough that he was satisfied with his diagnosis, so he sat my parents and me down for a chat. "I always suspected that the first surgery on Walt's legs would not be sufficient to solve his walking difficulties. Without feet, Walt's weight, which, I am sorry to say, is becoming considerable, is all focused on a small point on the ball at the end of the leg. As you get heavier, Walt, your legs are bowing, thus making it difficult for you to walk."

"What can be done about this?" my mom asked. I didn't want to hear the answer because I knew I'd be the one going through the hardship.

"I see no other option; we have to operate. This time we won't affect the ankles like the first time. This time we will surgically break the tibia and control the regrowth with pins."

"When does this need to happen?" Mom asked

"Let's see. He's in the third grade now, right? No need to interrupt the fine educational process until we must. We can wait and operate in early summer. The pins will have to stay in for a while, and then we'll remove them, put casts back on his legs, and let them finish healing. Figuring time for him to learn to walk again, I'd say we're looking at a six-month process. Sorry to put you through this, Walt, but if we do it now, you should be able to walk without corrective surgery again." I knew Dr. Bankston was doing this because it was going to help me, but I remembered not being able to walk from before. I didn't like being in a wheelchair. Getting anywhere becomes such an ordeal for everyone. I hated being patted on the head and being reassured by people who have no idea what they're talking about that all would be better soon.

"I can see you're reluctant," Dr. Bankston added. "I'm sure this is a very unpleasant process for you. What I need you to consider is I'm trying to help your legs, so you can walk when you're my age and beyond. Real fixes take real work. We can do our best to solve this now, or you can let another doctor do it when you're ready to meet some pretty girl at the end of a church aisle. Your choice."

One of the many things I loved about Dr. Bankston was that he seemed to believe in a future for me. My own parents were reluctant to even consider that I might grow into a man, but my doctor believed someone might be able to love me, even grow old with me. That was very powerful. He not only believed I'd be able to walk; he showed me glimpses of the world into which I'd walk.

We all agreed on the surgery, and I went back to pretending I was just like any other third-grader. One day in Mrs. Parsons' class, an odd-looking pale-skinned boy with dark hair and dark-rimmed glasses walked up to me as if he were going to speak. No one ever spoke except teachers, so I stopped what I was doing and looked up. He was with a chubby blond boy. Both were smiling, which made me suspicious.

The dark-haired boy was the first to speak. "We were told in first grade by our teacher that we shouldn't talk to you. She said you had a disease and it would be wrong to tease you. What do you have?"

"I don't have a disease."

"Told ya," the chubby blond said. "They would never allow some sick kid to sit in class with us. We could all get it."

"There's nothing to get. I'm not sick."

"What's your name?" the dark-haired boy asked.

"Walt Nelson. What are your names?"

"Danny and Chuck. I'm Dan," the dark-haired boy answered.

"Do you like to read?" Dan asked. "We are big sci-fi fans personally. I guess you know what sci-fi is?"

I wasn't even sure what he was yet. I was just glad to interact with two people in my class! They could become friends. I was very excited.

"Yes, it's science fiction. My dad and I watch 'Star Trek' every time it comes on." This was true. In spite of all that divided us, we could agree on watching Kirk and the boys.

"I have to admit that is science fiction, but it is sci-fi at its most basic level," said Dan. "Real sci-fi should go deeper than just spaceman encounters aliens. Aliens attack. Spaceman kills aliens. You need to read some Isaac Asimov, Arthur C. Clarke, Robert Heinlein and maybe some fantasy as well like J.R.R. Tolkien. Have you read any of these writers?"

"Did you know John Lennon said the Beatles are bigger than Jesus? What do you think of that?"

"Who is John Lennon?" I asked the dark-haired inquisitor.

"We should be friends. You need our help."

By the end of the school year, I was reading science fiction and I had discovered a love of biographies. When I look back on the third grade I don't think of it as an extraordinary year, but it was the year with Dan and Chuck's help that I learned to read. The last book our teacher read us was "Charlotte's Web." I tried hard to listen as she read to us, but I couldn't. I kept thinking about the surgery I'd face after school let out for the summer. As the book drew to its conclusion, suddenly everyone was crying. The book was ending sadly, although I wasn't listening and didn't know why. I found myself crying, too – not for a kind, insightful spider, but for a boy who was afraid to be turned into an invalid. I looked around the room and wondered how they had mustered sympathy for a character in a book when I was about to have both of my legs surgically broken, and no one talked with me about it. I dried my tears. I didn't know it, but I was soon to learn how not to cry.

Once again, I was in the children's ward at Vanderbilt Hospital. There was a herd of child patients sharing the room, with parents and grandparents coming and going more frequently than hospital staff. The sound level was at the same decimal level as an airport runway. My bed was in the corner of the room across from the door. No one could sneak up on me from behind, and I always knew who was entering the room. I thought I was safely positioned. I was wrong.

A couple of hours after I had settled in for the afternoon, a boy named Bobby took the bed beside mine. We were both 8; my 9th birthday would come a few days after my surgery; we were both boys; and we both were facing surgery. The similarities stopped there. He was hell in pajamas, and he never took prisoners. He wanted me to play cards. No, I have trouble holding cards. I don't care for card games. Did I want to race down the hallway? No, I am here to get my legs fixed. I walk badly and seldom run. Did I want to trade dinners? No, they were the same. Have I ever swallowed poison? No. He had. That's why he was there. To make sure he'd live. Why did you …? Hey, you won't play games, so I won't answer your questions. This back-and-forth continued until he asked if I wanted some water. I was lying in my bed with my back to him. I didn't want any water and I told him so.

Bobby was standing in the bed adjacent to mine. He gleefully shouted, "Boy, I've gotta pee!" and held a pitcher of water over my body and began pouring a small, steady stream on my side. I jumped, fearing the worst, but it was only water.

"Stop it!" I shouted. Then he tossed the pitcher in such a way that a sheet of cold water formed in the air over me and settled upon me like an anti-blanket whose evil purpose was to keep me awake all night, so I would feel even worse going into surgery tomorrow. "You didn't drink poison, someone tried to poison you, didn't they?" I screamed, more shocked and colder than angry.

The nurses moved Bobby to another bed, in a private room, for the night. Lesson learned: if you want your own room in a hospital and can't afford one, act like a jerk. Got it; bad behavior is rewarded. Then the nursing staff went to work trying to keep me healthy so my legs could be broken tomorrow without delay. My sheets were changed, and I was switched into a hospital robe that was open in the back. My grandmother, who was staying with me that evening, was sleeping when Bobby launched his offensive but was now fully awake and in grandmother mode assured me no one would see my backside and they would change me into this hospital gown before the surgery anyway. Finally, I accepted the inevitable, rolled up in my sheets and got brief snippets of sleep.

I awoke the next morning to Bobby's parents talking. "We have no idea what that boy was thinking," his father was saying. "I hope you got some sleep." I wanted to tell him I'd have gotten more if he'd shut up, but Marine sons don't talk that way. The mother offered to buy me new pajamas, a toy from the gift shop, books, magazines – whatever would distract me from wanting to kill her precious little boy.

My parents entered then. It was clear the sergeant had been apprised of the situation; he set up a perimeter and took charge immediately. "I'm sure Walt is fine. A little water never hurt anyone. The nurses must prep him for surgery, so let's step aside and let them do their work. Show them what a Nelson is made of, son. Be tough in the operating room. No crying. We'll be here when you get out."

I couldn't help but wonder if he and mom had really come all the way to Nashville early this morning just to clear the way for the nurses and tell me not to cry. Dad never liked messes, so I'm sure he would long be proud of the work he did here today.

No one seemed to worry that I might be scared or in need of some comfort. My dad had broken bones before, so I thought maybe he had brought Mom to give me the moral support he didn't get when he broke his back.

They came for me as I was struggling against the medication they had given me to make me sleep. I began to wave about frantically and cry. I'm not sure if I was reaching for or pushing against something. I just wanted someone to tell me it was going to be all right. When I arrived in the operating room, most of the actions were a blur. I was switched to the operating table, and IVs were attached to my arms. A mask fitting over my mouth and nose emitted one of the foulest odors I'd ever know. I was instructed by Dr. Bankston, who as the superstar of the room was last to arrive, to count backward from 100. While I did so, my vision began to blur. I found myself blinking, as if I wanted to clear my eyes of this scene and awaken to a better one. The blinks were slowing down when I heard the word, "Scalpel."

"NO!! I'm not asleep!" I screamed at the top of my lungs.

Dr. Bankston laughed. "You must like the sleeping gas we're giving you because now we have to start all over again putting you to sleep." I had to start the countdown again, and when somewhere off in a hospital-induced mental fog I heard the spirit of the word scalpel hauntingly float between this dimension and the next, I stayed quiet and waited for the vision to begin.

# CHAPTER TWELVE
## Recovery

I arrived at the hospital feeling fine; I returned home broken, sore and unable to walk. It is hard to understand the wheelchair experience until one has endured it for a substantial amount of time for one's self. The self-propelled, comfortable chairs of today aren't even the descendants of the uncomfortable dinosaurs we had in the 1960s. The seats were hard, with a leathery covering and a bit of foam underneath to tease the ass into believing it will be treated kindly. The wheels were perpendicular to the floor with little traction because everyone knew wheelchair riders had nowhere important to go. To fold these chairs required the dedication of a committee of people, an Act of Congress and a special dispensation from God. Once folded, the chair barely fit into a car trunk, which further discouraged a person with a disability to want to ever leave the house.

The day after I came home, I got a surprise visit from several members of my third-grade class. This group was headed by Dan and Chuck, my buddies. They brought me numerous gifts; most of them mysteriously were books Dan thought I should read. I had never had a group come together to celebrate anything for me before. We were not a birthday-party family. Once, when I was 5, I asked for a birthday cake. My mom got me one with a cowboy on it. It was the coolest-looking cake I would ever receive, but only family members were invited to share it.

They made it very clear they couldn't stay long, and as it was difficult to get me across our house's threshold, we stayed on the porch for our visit. Beth joined us, but she had a distant look on her face. She had very little to say. My classmates asked about my surgery, and I got the distinct feeling she felt left out. When everyone left, I took some of the magazines and books I thought she'd like and offered them to her. She accepted them and added, "I had my tonsils taken out. I didn't get any gifts."

"Now you have some." She smiled as she rolled me into the house.

Frankie was 5 years old the summer after my surgery, and he was a sight to behold. He was a slender, blond, blue-eyed remake of my dad. Dad would claim he was that cute when he was Frankie's age, too. Some nights after dinner, the family would sit and watch to see what cute thing he would do. One night he entertained us by donning a hunting cap of my dad's and carrying a hunting boot by a shoestring. He wanted to be like my dad; Dad wanted to still be Frankie. I remember looking at Beth to reassure her that we all feel left out sometimes.

I, too, was my dad, but not the cute one. I wasn't the hunting cap, boot-carrying adorable remake. I was the hospital-bed Frank. I was the not-quite-whole one who expected his flaws to come cascading down on him in shame. These two were soon to meet and to be intertwined forever.

Dad was placed on third shift at work and left for work late in the afternoon and came home in the wee hours of the morning. That meant that we never saw him until the weekend unless we were in trouble. The tension between us that had begun to fade after the barn incident began to come back to us. While in bed at night, since I couldn't get out of bed on my own, I learned to sleep while ignoring the need to use the restroom and began wetting the bed. This was never intentional and there may have been other physiological factors at play here I do not know, but the bottom line was that I again, at the age of 9, became a bed-wetter, and the sergeant didn't like it. He first learned of the problem from my mom, who would change my sheets in the morning and wash the dirty ones. When Dad asked her why she insisted on doing so much laundry, she wasn't about to take the brunt of his anger, so she explained to him that I was wetting the bed. The next evening when Dad came home, he checked my sheets. They were wet, so he began shouting, "Why are you wetting your bed?" I was asleep and sat up quickly with the shouting.

"I didn't know until just now that I did."

"Don't talk back to me! I work hard every day so my family can have the things they need, and you're lyin' in your bed takin' pees because you're too lazy to piss in the jar your momma leaves you. Now, you're going to talk back to me, too?"

I stayed quiet. He leaned over to look in my eyes. "You keep this up, and you won't have a bed to sleep in. Keep going, and I'll throw you out of my house. Piss in your sleep after that and I guess I'll have to choke the piss out of you. Do you understand?"

"Yes, sir."

"I CAN'T HEAR YOU!"

"Sir, yes, sir!"

"You better sir-yes-sir me. I'll crack your head open like a melon. Ain't nuthin' in it anyway." Dad punched the wall above me for emphasis and went to bed. Amazingly, he was snoring within 10 minutes. I was awake the rest of the night. I was afraid I'd fall asleep and pee again.

The next morning at breakfast, I talked with Mom. "You know I'm not doing this on purpose." She said nothing. "Why is Dad getting so mad?"

"Your father is working hard right now and doesn't want to come home to problems like bed-wetting."

"Do I ever wake you in the night when it happens?"

"No."

"Do I wake you trying to get away from the wet bed?"

"No."

"Don't I just lie there quietly and tolerate wet sheets until morning?"

Her quick intake of air betrayed my dad's sneaking up on me. He slapped me hard against the back of my head. "If you have a problem with what I'm doing take it up with me." I turned toward him. I was afraid of what he'd do if I didn't. When I turned, Dad was standing there, nude. Either I'd made him so angry he didn't bother to dress before dealing with my insubordination, or he just didn't have enough respect for me to dress. Regardless, seeing my father nude and angry was a type of foreshadowing

I didn't want or need. He leaned toward me again. "You will do what I say when I say, whether you like it or not. Are we clear?"

"Sir, yes, sir."

"Atta boy!" He slapped the back of my head again, hard. "Now I'm going to sleep if this discussion is through." He walked his fat ass back to bed.

"Walt, you have to understand ..."

I rolled my chair away from the table and waited to go to my grandmother's house for the day.

For the next several nights, my dad and I replayed the same scene. He would come home, yelling, and I stayed quietly respectful. I really tried to stop the bed-wetting. I drank very little at night, hoping that would stop the problem. I took books to bed with me hoping to read all night, but that plan didn't work either. I tried sleeping sitting upright; I thought that sitting up would make my getting wet more uncomfortable and make me stop. After school started back, Dad began hanging my urine-stained sheets on the clothesline so kids on the school bus could see my sin. Nothing worked. I trained myself to awaken while peeing and stop, but I could never eradicate the problem altogether.

When it became clear his approach wasn't working, he changed it. He would enter my room quietly, check to see if the sheets were wet, then wrap his hands around my neck and wake me, choking me. He was a very strong man, and I knew if he really wanted to kill me, he would have crushed my neck and I would be gone. Instead, he wanted and succeeded in communicating to me his rage, his desire to be rid of me, his frustration with what he perceived as my insubordination, and I hated him for it. I awoke like this so many times I cannot count them. They did nothing to stop the problem. They taught me I had little worth and that I should be afraid.

After a few weeks of this it was time to go back to the doctor and have the pins removed. Both Mom and Dad took me, which was normal, but they kept looking at each other in a way that made me suspicious. When we arrived at the Junior League House, I was X-rayed to make sure the bones were healing nicely. There was no room in the house set aside for surgeries, but there was a room far enough away from the other day patients that they would be unable to hear any screaming coming from the room. There were some medical machines, a bed and the privacy needed to torture the young.

After the prep work, Dr. Bankston joined us. "Everything is looking good, Walt. We'll have you up and dancing in no time. If you'll remember, I told you before the operation that you'd have casts on your legs in two stages. We are going to remove these casts and the pins today. Then we'll recast your legs and let them finish healing. If everything goes as we suspect, you should be able to walk and go back to school after the holiday break."

"Do you have a rash, Walt?" he asked as he began to examine me.

"No, sir."

"Why is your neck so red and tender-looking?"

"I don't know," was my excuse.

"Frank, Linda, look at this. Have you seen this before?" All three adults were standing over me examining me like a science project.

An entire novel flashed in the faces of my parents in the brief seconds they glanced at each other. They both knew they were looking at the rub burns my Dad had made on my neck while choking me. Mom's face seemed to be afraid. She was worried that the dirty little family secret was about to burst into the open. Dad, as usual, was angry. Here this Vanderbilt doctor was about to interfere with the way he was raising his son. Both glances gave way to the subplots of Mom's inability to stop my Dad from performing his abusive acts on his child and my Dad's inability to ask Mom to make the bad dreams of his father's violence quiet themselves in his mind. So many unexpressed fears and anxieties dwelt in that small triangle of faces that the simple light of truth had no hope of abiding there. We should have had our faces framed there in a triangle with the word "Shame" written in the middle. It would have made a nice family crest.

"I don't know what the matter with him is," Dad offered. "It's always something. When was the last time you washed that neck?"

"Sir, I don't know, sir."

"Doc, can we get on with this?"

"Sure." Dr. Bankston was not one for giving up, but there were other matters at hand. Dr. Bankston turned to Mom and said "Linda, I believe you'd be more comfortable in the other room."

"I don't want to leave Walt. He might get scared."

"Do you remember when we drew blood from Walt in the hospital?" Of course, she did. I, it turns out, am a hard stick. When I was in the hospital before the surgery, a team came to my bed to draw blood from me. After trying a few times in the left arm, they tried a few in the right. When that didn't work either, they suggested the top of the thighs. They pulled my gown up to my lower stomach, leaving my privates covered, swabbed the area and tried another three times to draw blood. With each shot to the thigh, I released a blood-curdling scream that would have frightened any self-respecting banshee, and yet they kept trying. When someone suggested the other thigh, I surrendered my screaming for old-fashioned crying and Mom fainted and fell through the privacy curtain surrounding the bed. Mon was carried out of the room to recover, and I begged to go with her. Then Dr. Bankston arrived. I could tell he was about to tease me about raising hell when he took a good look at my bruised, swollen arms and thigh. "What the Hell are you fools doing?" he demanded. I had never seen him angry like this.

"We were drawing blood," an unlucky intern answered.

"Really? Where is it?" he asked. "Don't you mean you were failing to draw blood and in an attempt to cover your ineptness, you were torturing this child?"

"Not intentionally, sir."

"Go back to my office and wait for me there. Find a sheet of paper and the closest thing you can find to a crayon, and write over and over again, "Do no harm." Keep it up until I get there. Understood?"

"Yes, sir." The interns left. Dr. Bankston turned back to face me, swabbed my right arm in an untried spot, and quickly and painlessly drew the blood he needed.

I came back to the present with the buzzing of the saw that was beginning to open my left cast. Several strips were cut from the top of the cast below the kneecap to the base of the leg. Slowly the medical team began to remove the cast in strips, and as each cast was fully removed, they raised each leg upward in triumph, so I could see the legs with pins still protruding like limbs and small flakes of skin falling like autumn leaves. They lowered the legs and then Bankston gave an almost imperceptible signal and the team encircled me to hold me down. My father was assigned my shoulders; I could see his upside-down face looking grimly at me as he judged me through his thick-black Buddy Holly glasses. His glance told me that after surveying all that I am, he judged me lacking and was sentencing me to the pain I was about to receive.

Apparently, my small arms weren't perceived as a threat because nurses were asked to hold them. A doctor was placed at each thigh, and Dr. Bankston was to pull the pins while a colleague controlled the lower leg. I wish I had a picture of the wink Dr. Bankston gave me just as he began. I loved that man for rebuilding me and making so much of my life possible. Yet the wink he gave me signaled the last time I'd ever again have full and complete trust in him.

The first step was to clip the tips off the pins, so they could be pulled off through the legs without obstacle. Dr. Bankston had a pair of what looked like very powerful scissors, and the tips were doffed like rosebuds from a stem. Then he attached another instrument to the first pin and explained he would pull it out. The pins were to be extracted one at a time. He assured me that since a "local" had been shot into each leg, the pain should be deadened some. I was not comforted by the word "some." When he began to pull, it felt like what I must assume it would feel like to have a sword extracted from my side. I screamed and tried to break free. I was aware that I was making matters worse, but I didn't care; I needed this to stop. My father and the nurses looked like bad cowboys trying to stay on their horse. The pins kept coming and coming; there were only six. How could it hurt so long?

I began to wonder for what crime I was being punished. There were six pins, but seven deadly sins. Had I omitted one, or were they saving for a grand finale? No matter what I did, I could not get away. They kept telling me I was making things worse. But how do you submit to torture? I had to fight. It was all I had.

When Dr. Bankston switched to the second leg, I had a second to look around. For the first time, I realized my father's face was directly over mine. The look on his face ensnared me. He was crying, not silent tears at the end of a battle as he counted the dying. His were tears flowing through pain, crying as if the pins were being pulled from his legs. He let the scene of him having his back broken in the Marines come rushing through him, and he was a warrior again, he was baring his teeth and growling an angry howl that he would not endure this. He was a God and gods do not suffer pain! His tears ordered a halt, but doctors aren't Marines. The Hippocratic Oath hides behind "No harm": He could roar if he wanted – the pins must come out; I must walk again. The battle must continue, without the release of death. He looked down at me without words, and a single tear fell from his eyes into mine. For so many years he had told me not to cry, and today he cried for me. Without either of us moving, we stood together, wrapped arms around each other's shoulders and walked to a more peaceful knoll, and we sat. We looked out at the devastation together and cried. As he began to fade, I stood and returned to the table, lay back down, and waited together alone for the last pin to be pulled.

After the exorcism of the pins, new casts had to be put on my legs, so the healing could continue. They would be removed in three months. Dr. Bankston told me how proud of me he was and how bravely I endured the pain. He assured me pain is not long remembered, and it would be the joy of a life of walking I would most remember from this experience. For the first time in my young life, he was wrong.

# CHAPTER THIRTEEN

## Cold

My legs are somewhat coned-shaped, with large knees and legs that get thinner as they dwindle to the ankles. Most people are surprised to discover I have ankles. It is the actual feet I'm missing. No strange flat piece protruding from the leg with those dangling little shell-capped worms squirming at the end. Toes run the range of quite cute to horrifying, depending on the foot. One might think that since I have fingers, I'd feel comfortable with toes. I only have two fingers, so even they are a bit strange to me. I have always thought feet and hands look ridiculously crowded. With my left hand, there is a thumb, and all the way on the other side is my pinky. Plenty of room. All other hands and feet I've seen have been so packed together; I cannot imagine what you would do with those little things.

Since my legs were conical, it was vital that my new cast be shaped where the cast was slightly bent at the knee to prevent slipping. I was no Vanderbilt med student, but I could feel the cast slipping before we left for the long ride back to Clarksville. I kept mentioning this to the medical team as they were rolling me out of the facility and to my parents' car, but I assume no one wanted to let Dr. Bankston know they'd screwed up, nor did they want to admit that a 9-year-old boy realized a problem they hadn't anticipated, so I was reassured, packed into the car and sent home.

When we arrived home, my father unloaded the wheelchair from the trunk, picked me up, placed me in it and wheeled me to my room. After he lifted me from the chair and sat me in the floor, he took the unprecedented step of sitting down beside me. I really expected a "We shared a moment in that room today" speech about how he and I found common ground on the vast terrain of terror that was my experience that afternoon. Again, I was wrong.

"I have something I need to explain to you," Dad began. I couldn't possibly have been paying more attention. "Anytime you might decide you want to share the private things that go on between the members of this family with strangers like Dr. Bankston, you feel free to go ahead. If you do, you need to be prepared to take care of yourself because I won't spend a dime on you. Are we clear?"

"I didn't say anythi–"

"No, but you didn't mind showing your neck around the room either, did you?"

"But, Dad, I …"

"See, you can't open your mouth without challenging me."

"I'm just …"

He hit me in the upper arm so hard I was knocked over sideways. My casts clacked together loudly, and the newly wounded legs underneath were too sore to take the movement. I lay on my side, not moving or making a sound. My mother had started down the hallway to my room when she must have figured out what was happening and stopped. I was in as much of a fetal position as my casts would allow, and I was still and silent.

"Next time you feel like confessing, remember there are worse pains in the world than having pins pulled from your legs." When he had been crying over me at Dr. Bankston's office, I thought he had crossed some chasm that had been a barrier between us all my life, and now we would have a bridge to better understanding we could build together. Instead, he sat me back in an upright position and shook me vigorously like an Etch-A-Sketch so I would erase and the son he always wanted would appear in my place. When he shouted, "Will you keep your mouth shut or not?" I finally realized I could not give the answer he wanted. His real question was, "Would I always disappoint him?" How could I know? My silence satisfied him, and he went away.

After the removal of the pins, night times in the Nelson house did not improve. When I would lie down at night, the casts would slip from their usual place because the med student had forgotten to bend my knee. There was a narrow part of the cast designed to wrap around the area over the ankles. The ankle sections were too narrow to be comfortable on any other part of the leg, so if the cast slipped down, which it tended to do when I slept, it would restrict blood flow to the rounded ends of my legs. The longer the circulation was restricted, the more it would hurt. When I explained this problem to my parents, they would remind me that the casts were made by Vanderbilt med students who were smarter than I and capable at their chosen profession. So I stopped explaining and had another reason to dread nightfall.

Sleeping was difficult in these ill-fitting casts. I would fall asleep on my back, but shortly afterward I would try to sleep on one side, then the other. This would cause my casts to slip down, crush the bottoms of my legs, and I would awake crying. Usually, at first, my mom would come to my room to help me. She would gently ease the cast back into place and dry my tears. Then she would always ask, "What is the first thing you'll do when you can walk again?"

"Stand and give you a hug."

This made her smile. "You don't have to stand for that." She leaned over and hugged me.

"Thanks for helping me with the casts." I almost always was the one who signed off in my conversations with my mom.

One morning, a few weeks after I acquired my new casts, my dad joined us for breakfast. He normally slept until the afternoon, then awoke and got ready for work. He usually worked either the second or third shift, so we did not see him often. He made a special effort that morning.

"Do you have any idea how much you whimper at night?" He was talking to me, of course. "From the moment I enter the house, until I *finally* fall to sleep, you cry like a baby." I tried to explain why the braces were hurting me, but he wasn't interested. "I can't help your problem, but you are going to help me with mine. I must have sleep. At night, while you are beginning to moan, I'm at a factory running machines that could crush this house. If I fall asleep, or if my attention wanders, I could get a lot of men hurt. But I can't get a decent night's sleep because my son is in his room at night calling his other whale friends to come join him."

I could not feel shame for being in pain. I knew that's what he wanted from me, but I couldn't give it. Instead, I gave him the next best thing. Silence. He needed sound. He wanted to be certain I was registering what he was saying, so he punched me in the arm. I gritted my teeth but said nothing. "Do you understand what I'm telling you?"

"Yes, sir," I reassured him.

"Then explain it."

"When I cry in my sleep at night ..."

"I never said you were asleep!"

"I am. I often don't ..."

"Save that crybaby crap!" he screamed. "You are crying for attention! Doesn't your mother coddle you enough while you're awake? I don't know what you expect of us? Of course, casts are uncomfortable. When I broke my back as a Marine, I lay in a hospital bed for three months in excruciating pain. Do you think I lay in bed all night crying for the nurses? No, I didn't! I stayed quiet and wished I had died with the same dignity my men had when they hit the beach in Vietnam without me."

My dad took a moment to reflect on what truly was an amazing story. He had fallen into an above-ground shaft of a cave while on a night maneuver on the island of Okinawa. They were training to land in Nam. Dad fell and broke his back. His men went without him. They were all killed upon landing. I was his punishment for surviving.

"I don't know what game you're playing in there, and I don't care. The next night you disturb my sleep is the last time you sleep in my house." He got up from the table to go back to bed. Looking at my mom, he added, "See to it he sleeps somewhere else or is perfectly quiet. He won't like the alternative."

I sat in my wheelchair and worried all day that day. Where would Mom make me sleep? I really was crying in my sleep, so I didn't know how I could stop myself. When Mom got home from work, we talked about it. "Your dad was just tired this morning," she assured me. "He didn't mean it. This is your house, too. Just try to stay as quiet as possible, and you'll be fine." I was as skeptical as she was gentle. At bedtime, Mom got some extra blankets, rolled them and placed them under my legs. This kept the casts at an incline, and gravity should have helped my casts stay more in place and not hurt the end of my legs. It was the best idea I had heard, and I fell asleep thinking the problem was solved.

"Why are you in here!" my father was screaming as I awoke. I couldn't breathe, and it took me a moment to realize his hands were tightly wrapped around my throat. I have never before or since seen his face like that night. He looked like he was falling deeply into an abyss, with no hope of retrieval. He temporarily lost his mind. The look of madness was fodder for my nightmares well into adulthood.

He began shaking me around the bed, holding tightly to my neck. My casts kept clicking together so hard I thought they and my neck were racing to see which would break first. When he finally dropped me back onto the bed, he could see the burn marks he had left that were encircling my throat. Maybe for a second, he worried that someone would see the irritated skin like Dr. Bankston did. He didn't worry long. As I began to realize we were winding down, and I would not die that night, I looked toward the doorway of my room. There, standing vigil, was Mom, the silent sentinel to my suffering. I never blamed her for not stopping Dad. I knew she couldn't. Beth told me later that she lost respect for my mother because all she did was watch and cry. Beth was wrong. Mom gave me hope and kindness. I never doubted she loved me. She also taught me the horror of being powerless. I would spend my life trying to avoid that trap.

"See you again tomorrow night," Dad promised as he turned out the lights and went to bed. It turned out I had attempted to roll over and knocked the blanket off the bed. I didn't have to worry about repeating my mistake. There was no possibility of falling back to sleep after that scene.

The next evening, Mom and I had a foolproof plan. She would put two rolled blankets under my casts and put a rolled blanket on either side of me. I felt cocooned and unable to move in a way that would endanger me. I fell into a safe sleep.

When I awoke, I was rising into the air. In a second, I saw I was being lifted by my dad. His face seemed calm and resolved not to look into mine. I immediately began to worry where I was being taken, but I knew better than to ask. He carried me from my room, down a hallway, through the kitchen and the living room. Then he opened the door into the side lawn. There was a rather steep hill between the house and the fenced-in field where the cattle grazed. When he opened the door, snowflakes were falling from the late-night sky. A half an inch of snow covered the ground, and after Dad took a few steps up the hill he planted my formerly warm bottom in it. He turned to go inside and said, "You can cry all you want out here. There's no one who'll hear you. You can get your screaming all out of your system or freeze to death. I don't care which."

I was incredulous when he closed the door. He had done so before, while I stood in a dark barn stall, but out in the elements like this was beyond comprehension. I found a scream inside of me that must have been heretofore unknown to children my age. It was the scream of a bayonetted soldier who realized he'd die in a malaria-infested forest-hell. It was the scream of a French royal watching the guillotine blade drop. It was waking to find death standing between you and the bedroom door and you are the only one he has come to retrieve. The worst part of my situation was that on a cold winter night in Tennessee, one does not freeze instantly, and in that horrible note lies all hope as well.

I screamed for my mom to come and get me. She didn't. I pleaded for Beth to help. She never stirred. My grandparents were a tenth of a mile away. God was making snow. There was no one who'd help. When I accepted this, I slowed down and then stopped screaming. For the first time that night, I began to look around me. Although it was quite late at night, the moon hidden behind the clouds sent through enough light to make the surroundings look like it was almost daybreak. I also realized that my dad's emotions were hot; his hands burned my neck, and his face was always contorted with the heat of his temper. Here everything was cool and calm. It was a fine time to think and reflect. The reflective white of the snow seemed to cover the dirty normalcy of nature and promised purity worthy of a redeemed soul. It was precisely at that moment, looking at the snow, that I wasn't really that cold. I was wet and uncomfortable but not frozen by defeat. I wiped my tears for the last time until I had my own children. Tears are fuel for anger like gas for a fire. I would stop giving Dad what he wants. If he needed a symbol for his own shame, he would have to find his own. My body was incomplete, but not disabled. I would live beyond this night and beyond my fear of him. I just had to remind myself that it really wasn't that cold, and maybe my challenges would be surmountable. As my body temperature began to drop, snowflakes stopped melting on my sleeves and hair. Just as I was musing that for the first time in my life, I was beginning to blend in, the side door opened. I believe I caught a look of surprise on Dad's face when he saw I was snow covered. He asked if I was ready to come back in. I hesitated and responded, "If you are ready for me." He sensed my new spirit of defiance, but we never spoke of it. That would have been a victory for me and a defeat for him. Marines never admit defeat, but occasionally they do lose. From that night until this, I have never given in to the idea of cold. I have one winter coat that I wear only in extreme winter weather. When people ask me if I'm not cold, I smile and say, "There is no cold." This was the end of my night attacks from my dad, but I never really learned to sleep again.

## CHAPTER FOURTEEN
# Back to School

I sat in my uncomfortable wheelchair looking out of the window facing the front yard of the Sullivan house. While Mom and Dad worked during the day, Frankie and I stayed with Grandma Sarah. Their house was a simple six-room house, with the bathroom added on when I was a baby. Except for that room, Granddaddy Walter had built this house and was proud of it. Outside the front window, I could see Frankie swinging his 5-year-old body from tree limb to tree limb as I sat there, stationary, joyless.

She was there before I noticed her. She watched me from the entranceway of the room. Then she slipped over to my chair and looked out the window over my shoulder. When I turned to see her face, I knew at once I didn't recognize her, but I instantly liked her. I'm not sure if it was her face, wrinkled and stretched by time and ages of smiling, or that she was too close to me and didn't seem to care. Whatever the reason, I felt like I was in the presence of someone who wanted to be there.

"Who are we watching in the tree?" was her first question to me. Not her last.

"That's my brother, Frankie."

"It's not fair, is it?"

"What?"

"That he can swing from the trees and you're stuck inside in this chair."

"I don't think about it much."

"Well, I'm glad to see that," she added, mysteriously.

"See what?"

"That you aren't a good liar. Your ears light up red as a stoplight. What would you say if I offered you something better than trees?"

"What's better than trees?"

"Books! With a good book, you are never limited in where you can go. With books, no one must fold or unfold your chair, push you or help you up or down stairs or ramps. With books, you can go anywhere you want, any part of the universe, see anything you want, speak any language and be home by dinner. Let me help you become a great reader, and you will never face an unconquerable obstacle again." She pulled up a chair but never asked me to turn away from the window and face her. I chose to do that on my own. Her name was Mrs. May Ella Upshaw. She was the sister-in-law of my first-grade teacher. She was assigned to be my homebound teacher; because of some bureaucratic snafu, she has been recently assigned to keep me caught up this semester, and the semester was nearly over. She assured me we were smart enough to get caught up, and we began to do so immediately. If I did well with my work, she rewarded me by leaving me with a book I could read. Books were rewards and since I had very little else to do, I read and learned. I explored space, traveled through history and discovered new worlds I'd never have heard of in Clarksville.

Mrs. Upshaw was the first teacher to work with me one on one. She questioned and pushed me. She challenged me and never took "No" for an answer. While we worked in that living room, just the two of us, I couldn't hide behind anyone else's answers. I had to give my own. Mrs. Upshaw was the Michelangelo who carved Walt the intelligent person out of the unshaped blob of disability Frank had considered him; I would forever be so indebted to her for what she did for me that I would spend over 30 years of my life attempting to do it for other kids.

When January arrived, I was walking again, timidly, but on my own.

I took the bus as usual and arrived for my first class just a few minutes before it started. The doorway into the classroom was down two steps, an unnecessary obstacle I didn't anticipate. As I surveyed the downward steps, I caught the attention of the waiting class, who got out of their seats and came to the doorway to greet me.

I told them I had missed them and was glad to be back. "Who can't tell a lie, Mrs. Upshaw?" I mused. They offered me hands to help me down the steps, which I refused, and we settled into our seats and school began. I soon discovered that except for math, I was ahead of the class! The lessons I still had to learn were not academic but social. One day I was in the restroom after lunch, and as I was washing my hands, some boys began to gather around behind me. The leader said, "Look boys, the crippled kid is washing his nub (a pejorative term used for my handless arm). The teachers act like he's something special. Let's kick his special ass." As he stepped toward me, I cupped my arms under the faucet in such a way that it shot water out and hit the leader in the crotch of the pants. He started frantically trying to dry himself off, and I ran from the room as fast as my newly healed legs would wobble me. Somehow, my teacher found out that I sprayed a boy with the faucet, and she was mad at me. Without asking what had happened, she stood me in front of the class and asked me to give her my hand turned palm side up. She picked up a wooden ruler and gazed into my eyes. After years with a Marine, this was nothing. I said, "Are you sure you want to strike the only hand I have with a wooden ruler?" She hesitated, and I knew I had already won. She stared deeply into my eyes, trying to discern whether I was bluffing about the damage hitting my hand might cause. Of course, I never said it would cause any damage; no lie was told. She finally let a smile break her stare. She couldn't and wouldn't hit me. I resolved right then and there to give her no reason to regret backing down.

One day, several weeks after I started back, I found myself on the playground. I was worried about being on such unsafe ground for me, but as soon as I had gone outside, I spotted a boy in my class who was new that year, but no one was talking to him. No one ever seemed to talk with him. This was familiar, so I approached him to talk.

"Hi. What's your name?" I was destined to be a journalist.

"Stephan, what's yours?"

"Walt. I never see anyone talking with you. Are you shy?"

"No, it's just that no one wants to be my friend."

"Why is that? Do you have cooties?" He laughed at that.

"No, they don't like me because I'm a Jewish."

"So what?" I had never read anything anti-Semitic in my life. There were very few Jewish people where I grew up, and I had never heard of anyone discussing them in my life.

"They believe Jews killed Jesus, so they don't like me."

"Wasn't Jesus Jewish?"

"Yes."

"Weren't the Romans the ones who actually put him to death?"

"Yes, but some Jewish religious leaders asked for it."

"Were you there?"

"No," he smiled.

"Did you want Jesus killed?"

"No!"

"How was any of this your fault?"

"It wasn't."

"I have no problems being your friend." We shook on it, but as life would have it, Stephan's dad was transferred up north. I was again the only single silhouette on the playground.

# CHAPTER FIFTEEN
## Doug Waters

The summer of 1969, shortly after my surgery, my parents let me stay up all night and watch the most amazing thing I'd ever seen on TV. I watched Neil Armstrong and Buzz Aldrin land on the moon! NASA had responded to President Kennedy's challenge to send men to the moon, and we as a nation learned a lesson that we would soon forget: Together, there is nothing we can't achieve. I remember watching them hop around the moon, wishing Earth had that same weak gravity. Even in those impenetrable suits, the astronauts' joy could not be contained. If they had stared carefully enough back at the Earth, I'm pretty sure they would have seen me smiling back at them.

The following spring, I saw the second most miraculous sight I'd ever seen. My parents and I were sitting on the front porch. Dad was reading the paper. Mom and I were talking. It was a lazy afternoon, when suddenly, I thought I was looking at me in an alternate universe. A car pulled up in front of my parents' yard, and out stepped what I at first assumed was a long-lost brother. He had hair like my Dad, short dark and curly, and a hand and leg prostheses like mine. He walked smoothly and rapidly (two things I've never accomplished) up the hill that is my parents' lawn to the porch. He introduced himself as Doug Waters and asked if he could sit and talk a moment. I couldn't help but stare. I had never seen anyone with limbs similar to mine.

After a few introductory remarks to my parents, he turned his attention to me. "Hi, Walt. As I mentioned a moment ago, I'm Doug. I work with your dad, but I'm here to talk with you."

"You have a hand like mine," I muttered.

"That's right," he confirmed, "and our legs are similar." He pulled his pants legs up and let me see that he wore the prosthetics of an above-the-knee amputee on each leg. I asked the question every amputee receives.

"What happened?"

That kind image of a possible Walt of the future smiled while answering me. "I'm going to help you with that question. I bet you get it a lot, don't you?"

"Not really. Most people just assume and don't talk to me at all."

"Well, when you're older, you'll get it a lot. When you do, tell people nothing happened that didn't happen to them. Tell them your parents had a baby, and that baby was you. Nothing went wrong: You aren't broken or defective. People want to hear about some terrible tragedy because an otherwise beautiful baby wouldn't be born so tragically disfigured. Come here, please," he waved me over to him. I stood and walked over. "Shake hands with me please." I only had one to offer him, so I raised it and his hand shaped like mine greeted me. Both hands were C-shaped, and our shake lacked the complicated fingers surrounding fingers complexity most hands deliver. Our shake was made of two hands coming together, with fingers contacting palms and backs of hands. Our shake was less clingy, less co-dependent.

"See," he was saying. "We can shake as men. We are born, grow up, go to school, marry, work, retire and die just like any man. So when they ask you 'What happened?' ask them the same."

"I will," I promised before I glanced and saw the uncomfortable look on my dad's face.

"I didn't just come here to show you how to shake; I came to ask you a question," he began, getting to his mission. "How would you like to go to a camp for people like us? By us, I mean the physically and mentally unique. It's called Easter Seals Camp, and it's in Mount Juliet, Tenn., across Old Hickory Lake from the Boy Scout Camp."

"What's the camp like?" I wondered aloud.

"It's full of kids like you who, just like you, have probably not met many kids like you before. There'll be lots of types of kids and counselors who may wear prosthetics, who may be missing legs, arms, noses, etc. There'll be people using crutches, wheelchairs, canes, service dogs, walkers, and there'll be people with various types of intellectual disabilities. The most important thing is there will be a bunch of kids, like you, who need to have a good time. So, what do you say, sports fan? Want to go to camp?"

Frank had had enough of not being the center of attention. "Hold on. We haven't discussed cost. You may be making promises my wallet can't keep."

"Not to worry, Frank. I have that all worked out. The Easter Seals Society has friends who set up scholarships for kids like Walt whose parents could use some help. This was the first time it dawned on me that my family didn't have much money. My medical care concerning my disabilities was provided by the Shriners of Nashville and the Junior League. They also gave me access to Dr. Bankston and the reconstructive surgeries. I knew these things and I was grateful, but I didn't know it was charity. The mighty Master Sergeant Frank Nelson received charity. Many people needed help. I understood that and respected it. Many things can happen in life that can cause a family to need help. But Frank the mighty, Frank the invincible needed help. Did he mind that I'm discovering this? Well, Dad, welcome to being human.

"What sort of things will we do at the camp?" I asked, eager for details.

"We may have a convert," Doug said with a smile. "We camp, fish, hike, swim, shoot rifles and bows and arrows, canoe, sing, eat and sleep just a little. Does any of that sound good to you?" I admitted it did.

"I'll leave the applications for you and your parents. Here's my card if you need any help. I'll be at the camp with you, but I won't necessarily be your counselor. They are all good though, so that won't be a problem, will it?"

I assured him it wouldn't. Doug rose, shook my parents' hands, shook my hand and walked back to his car.

"One more thing, Walt!" he shouted from his car. "Be prepared. This will change your life."

Not a moment too soon, I thought to myself.

# CHAPTER SIXTEEN
## Easter Seals Camp

When I got out of my parents' car, I was amazed at the sight in front of me. I saw the most varied assortment of people I'd ever seen in my life. There were moms, dads, sisters, brothers, aunts, uncles, cousins, husbands, wives, partners, friends and enemies. There were people from many parts of the globe; there were a variety of races, ethnicities, languages, and clothing styles. There were prosthetics, walkers, wheelchairs, canes, missing limbs, blind and deaf people, and equipment I couldn't identify. I was suddenly feeling a little fear. I didn't know my surroundings for the first time since I was hospitalized, and I feared this would be equally unpleasant.

I got out of the car to discover my parents were finishing paperwork. I was officially a camper. I got some T-shirts with "Easter Seals Camp" on them. I was given a card with the name of the cabin and wing where I'd stay, and it had the name of my counselor. His name was Martin, and he was a student in a University in Tennessee. I didn't know what a counselor was, so I really didn't care. We found my cabin, which really wasn't a cabin so much as a rancher with two large rooms on each side joined by bathrooms in the center and a foyer with an office for the head resident near the front door. We entered the front door and passed the office to find I was in the wing on the right. Someone told me to pick a bunk and settle in. I found an empty one near the middle of the room, claimed it, and Mom helped me unpack. The whole time, I kept noticing the array of different people around me. Every physical disability one could imagine was there on display. There were missing limbs, under-sized limbs, nonfunctioning limbs, and burned limbs. There were blind, and deaf kids. There were intellectually disabled kids, and I didn't understand what they were doing or saying. I felt three things with which I have since had to come to terms. All three of these things were things that as an adult, I would urge people to get past:

1. I was uncomfortable.
2. I wanted to go back home.
3. I felt sorry for the kids I saw around me.

I didn't realize it, but my life view was about to change.

Mom and Dad were expecting me to be afraid, and after a very brief attempt to reassure me, they got back in their car and returned home. It was just a few seconds before my counselor, Martin, gathered his campers together to meet. With Martin, there were five of us. I had leg prosthetics and no hands, a boy named Tom seemed to be quadriplegic. He used a wheelchair and showed no ability to use his legs. One boy's disability was invisible, and the fourth wore braces made of metal and circular bands and used crutches. Martin was a twenty-something, thin, dark-haired, pale-skinned Vanderbilt student. He had us introduce ourselves and then reviewed a few rules.

"I try to get to know my campers individually, so I may give each of you a task we can do together to get better acquainted. Would that be all right?"

We all agreed it would. Then Martin offered us a tour of the camp. It was laid out essentially in a circle. The main office building and chow hall was at 6 o'clock around the circle. Going clockwise, the two boys' dorms were at 8 and 10 o'clock. The boat dock was at noon. The two girls' dorms were at 1 and 3 and the craft building, which was an open-aired, single-walled building with a roof and concrete floor, was at 5. A hill dominated the center of the circle. It was crowned with a swimming pool. We walked the circle a couple times to make sure we knew where everything was. Punctuality was stressed. Being late often meant everyone had to wait, and campers had ways of correcting you if you made them wait too much. The camp was round and protective like a fort, but it was warm, and kind like a hug. Martin's campers were happy with what they saw.

After our tour we returned to the cabin and washed up for dinner. Our meals were served on plates already placed on the tables when we arrived. Servers walked around offering seconds. Campers from each cabin wing sat together at first, but then they shifted around as other friends were made. Counselors sat at the ends of tables, like substitute parents, and most fed campers in their group who needed assistance. Martin fed Tom, who was quadriplegic. Tom could move his arms around a bit, but not enough to help him feed himself. I asked Martin, "If Tom's a quadriplegic, why can he move his shoulders?"

"Maybe you should ask Tom," Martin suggested.

"I have what's known as 'incomplete quadriplegia.' I can move my shoulders and biceps, but not much more," Tom answered with the practice of a person who has lived with a disability for a lifetime. I started to ask how he became a quadriplegic, but he seemed to be enjoying his meal, so I stopped.

After the meal concluded, we had free time that night, so I put up my tray and hung around the chow hall looking for something to do. Already on the first day, people were pairing up or settling into groups of three or more. They were fanning out, mostly girls' and boys' groups, but there were some couples already developing. I had assumed that we would divide by disability. That was not the case. I wondered what these groups found in common. I also wondered why I wasn't in a group yet.

"Hey, Walt!" It was Martin shouting to me while pushing Tom's chair. "Tom's going to help me walk off dinner. Want to go?"

"Sure!" I caught up with them and we began walking around the camp counterclockwise; this direction would send us in the direction of the girls' cabins first. As we began walking, it was Tom's turn to start asking questions. He asked about my hand and lack of feet. I told him that once my doctor at Vanderbilt asked me if I wanted to know why I was born with my lack of limbs. Of course, I did; it was one of the most important questions of my youth. When dealing with disabilities, it is very hard to concentrate on why until you've spent quality time considering how. When he started to explain it to me, I saw my mother from just over his shoulder. She had a look on her face I did not know. She looked like a deep, dark secret that she had forgotten even existed was about to be revealed, and she did not want that to happen. Did she know why I was born with a disability? If so, why hadn't she ever told me? Were she and my father hiding something about my past? We lived our lives like pioneers on the prairie. Every time we saw strangers on the horizon, we circled the wagons and prepared to fend them off. We didn't trust the strangers and didn't like each other. We were at odd family, happy only in the emptiness a prairie could offer.

I told the doctor after considering the matter, maybe I shouldn't know why I was this way. "I need to focus on today and tomorrow. Yesterday has passed." It was weak dialogue, but he and my mom bought it. She looked relieved, he moved on, and I had no answers to the biggest question of my life.

"You still haven't found out?" Tom was clearly unhappy with my story.

"Not yet, but I hope to find out someday. The doctors have done a lot for me though. I can't be too disappointed. At least I can feed myself, dress myself and walk." I said this last part with all the youthful thoughtlessness I could muster.

Martin began rolling Tom's chair a little faster and faster, undoubtedly so I wouldn't be beside Tom when I said my next stupid and insensitive thing. When we got back to our cabin, it was time to wash our faces and brush our teeth. After I took my turn, I sat on the porch looking at the sky. Sometimes I felt as far away from others as these stars. It wasn't until I made my careless statement that I realized I was pushing away, not the others. It was so hard to relate to them. They were so … *handicapped*. I wanted to help and understand, but I just hurt and pushed away. I had plenty of time to think about it while I lay awake, listening to a large room full of kids whispering and snoring.

Something was banging, banging on the foot of my metal cot, and I sat up quickly to see Tom slamming my cot with his wheelchair, gleefully. "Morning, sleepyhead!" I thought I'd overslept, and looked around the room, expecting jubilant faces to be staring at me, laughing at my slothfulness. Instead, except for the two or three boys stirring because of the noise Tom was making, everyone else was still asleep. The outdoors showed signs of an awakening sun, but the leaves were not green lights signaling the world to, "Go!" They were dark leaves quietly rustling while the raven slept.

"Everyone is still asleep. Why are you waking me?"

"I want you to take me for a walk around the camp before breakfast."

"You woke me up to take you for a walk?" I asked, dryly.

"Yes," without worry. "Want to go?"

I stood, dressed, did what I needed in the restroom, and took the back handles of his chair and took him onto the porch. Mornings are beautiful things that should be videotaped and shown to people later during the day, but we were up now, and not enjoying it seemed a waste. "Which way, sir?" I used my best Cockney accent.

"To the left, Jeeves," he chuckled as we got underway. It was going to be a beautiful day. The sky was a perfect baby blue, soft and cloudless. As we rounded the western edge of the circle, Old Hickory Lake came into view. There is something magical about seeing a large body of water in the morning, with waves skittering about like insects that have found food. Oceans, lakes, rivers and streams all remind the introspective observer that there are many mysteries we do not understand. There are many things we have not seen.

The boat dock was down a winding path we were about to approach. It wasn't much of a dock. It was "T" shaped with most of its trunk cut away. A short walk took the pedestrian from the shore to a pier with a railing surrounding it on three sides and with a place filled with a houseboat on the right side. It provided a safe-enough place for campers to fish and launch canoes or load the houseboat. It was a magnet for those who needed to think. They would look over the side and see their reflections, hoping the small waves would turn their faces into answers.

We arrived at the small walkway that led to the dock. "Turn my chair to face the dock and lock it, please," Tom asked of me.

"What are you going to do?" I asked.

"I need you to leave me here for about 20 minutes," he requested.

"Let me get this straight. I got out of bed early this morning so you could be alone?"

"Sounds about right ..."

I didn't know how to respond to this, so I took off walking and did as he asked. While I passed the girls' cabins, I could hear water falling in the showers. I tried to imagine how wonderful it was in those rooms, but I couldn't. I walked past the arts-and-crafts center, and the counselors were ending a staff meeting. Martin came over to make sure I was OK. I explained why I was up, and he asked if I wanted him to get Tom. I assured him we would be at the chow hall in time for cleanup. He smiled, said, "Be a reliable friend!" and went back to the cabin. I walked the long way around by our cabin to get back to the boat dock. When I arrived, Tom was holding a pad of paper in his arms. He was also holding a pencil in his mouth. I walked up behind him, and on the pad, Tom had drawn a remarkable drawing of the dock and lake. The scale was believable, the shading was excellent, and he had framed the scene with water, vegetation and sky like a seasoned artist. After he finished, he bit the bottom right corner, tore the page from the pad with his mouth and tilted his head backward, offering me the page. I took it and spent several minutes admiring his work, and then I looked at him, told him what a great job he had done, then asked what he was trying to say.

"Next time you start feeling sorry for me, remember, I'm better than you are!"

We both laughed awkwardly, and I knelt beside him and we discussed the drawing in some detail. Then he told me to keep it. "Next time you see a kid who looks around the camp and acts like he is the only non-disabled kid in sight, give him this drawing, remind him he is one of us, too, and remind him he'd be lucky to be as talented as I am."

"I didn't realize I was being so weird. I've just never been with such a large number of kids with disabilities before."

"Do you find yourself feeling sorry for them? Or do you think that at least you aren't as bad off as some kids?"

"Yes." I was ashamed to admit it, but I had had both feelings.

"Everyone's journey is different. You just can't compare your disability with someone else's. You were born with yours, so when you see someone who had an amputation, you would be inclined to think you are better off. You don't have to adjust to limb loss, that's true, but you may have parts of your limbs that may get in your way, and if you had had an amputation, that issue could have been resolved. Besides, our physical selves aren't the point. I will never stand as tall as you, but I'm the smart one explaining things today. That means we are shoulder to shoulder."

"Yes, we are." I smiled and messed up his hair.

"Never mess up a quadriplegic's hair. It will force him to either run over you or wait until you are talking to a pretty girl, and roll by, fart, and blame it on you."

"It's going to be a difficult trip back to the cabin." When he started calling me curse words I had never heard before, I turned back and got him. I rolled him to his place at the table beside Martin. Martin asked if we had everything all worked out.

"I tried, but he's an idiot," Tom explained. Martin smiled and asked if I would like to feed my new friend. His waffle was delicious.

The next couple of days were "camp routine." We swam, fished, hiked, played various ball games, shot arrows with bows, and shot rifles. It was fun, and the summer days were more adventurous at camp. At the end of our third day, right after we had returned to the cabin from our dinner meal, I went out to the porch to find Martin sitting on the railing. He was looking off in space, but I was too young to give the guy some privacy.

"Hey, Martin."

"Hey, Walt. Everything OK?"

"I was about to ask you the same thing."

"Yeah, just thinking."

"What do you sophisticated Vandy students think about sitting on the railing of the front porch?"

"Speaking of Vandy, have you thought about whether or not you'd want to go to college?" With a steel-trapped mind like this, it would be a crime if I didn't go to college, I thought with a smirk on my face. I knew what he was doing, and he was not going to get away with it.

"I am asking what's on your mind, not mine."

"Well, Walt, I'm thinking about a woman."

"Do tell," I insisted.

"There's this lovely young woman who goes to Vandy with me whom I think is quite special." I guess Vandy people say things like "whom."

"Oh, thinking about a LADY," I sang in my nasal voice. "What's her name?"

"Margaret," he said with a smile.

"Why don't you call her up? Tell her you're thinking about her."

"No need to do that. She's down the street."

"Where?????!??" I asked.

"She's a cook in the chow hall."

"What's the problem? Dinner is finished. She should be finished with her job. Go talk to her!"

"It's not that simple. There are rules about "fraternizing" among the staff. Counselors are supposed to be with at least a camper all the time. We are here for you guys, not for sitting behind a tree with pretty women smooching or something."

"By the way, Martin, I have a problem. I haven't walked in ridiculous circles enough today. Why don't we go for a walk? I don't care if you want to bring a friend with you. What you do behind trees is none of my business."

"I could ask her," Martin grinned. "Sure, you wouldn't mind? I mean, technically, I'd still be doing my job."

"I don't mind at all," I assured him.

We walked to the chow hall, and Martin said he'd be right back. He slipped into an employees' entrance I had never noticed before. When he reemerged, he was accompanied by a woman who literally made my white, Middle Tennessean, overly-sheltered-from-life jaw drop to my chest. Margaret glided from the building like a dancer searching for her song. She was twirling around and messing up Martin's hair. He laughed and asked her to stop, but he didn't mean it. When she did, he introduced us.

"Margaret, this is Walt. He's one of my campers."

"I'm his favorite," I smiled, and we shook hands. She took my left hand in hers with confidence. She didn't seem awkward like most people do; she looked me in the eyes and shook. I looked into her eyes as well. It was the first time I had seen a black woman this closely. To call her black seemed too simplistic. Her skin was a potpourri of colors ranging from dark like the night to soft silky gold. Her hair was formed into an Afro, a popular style of the time, and I noticed her curls glistened in the sun. She had the strong broad nose of a queen that she claimed could smell bullshit a mile away, and her lips could make angels lean in for a soft kiss. If clothes had feelings hers might have intended to cover her curves, but they gloriously failed. At 10 years old, I would not have known this expression, but I know now that Martin and I, both, were out of our league. Fortunately for both of us, she could see our hearts and the walk was to continue.

We began our walk around the campus going to the east toward the girls' cabins first. Maybe we both wanted other women to see we could entertain an exquisitely attractive woman. Maybe they thought it would take both of us. I'll never know. Margaret danced-walked around the circle, and when she heard the song playing from a radio in the girls' cabin, she began singing, "It's Too Late" by Carole King. She would stop and hold Martin's hand until he snapped to a stop, spun and faced her. Her singing made even Martin forget the rules, and suddenly, one could see in his eyes that he and Margaret were all alone in a crowded world; she sang, he watched and although I shouldn't have been a voyeur on their private journey, I watched too. She was all grace and magic and was everything that is beautiful in the world. Martin hugged her many times on our walk. In my mind, I did, too.

When we came around to my cabin, I veered off unnoticed as the couple continued to the chow hall. Since there was no camper with them, they must have parted quickly because Martin was back and sitting beside me on the porch in no time.

"Thanks for walking with us," he said smiling.

"You're welcome."

"Hope you didn't peel away because you were uncomfortable."

"Not at all," I reassured him. "I just thought you could use a few seconds of privacy."

"What do you think of her?"

I didn't want to answer too enthusiastically, but I did want to be honest. "She is amazing. She is beautiful, sings and dances, and her eyesight is bad enough that she'll hang out with a cretin like you." Insults are a sure route for guys to become friends, and at that moment, Martin had let me in on his relationship and let me insult him. We were now friends.

"There are a lot of people who have given both of us a lot of grief for being together.

"Why?" I really wondered.

"Walt, there are many people out there who think whites and blacks shouldn't be together."

I know that's true, but I have never understood it. "Who could possibly meet Margaret and not fall in love with her?"

"You're not going to move in on my girl, are you?" He mockingly made fists and pretended to box with me.

"No, I'll stay back and leave you two alone, but only because I feel sorry for you." He gave me a fake swing to the jaw.

Maybe attending this camp should be obligatory, but you cannot help but look around you and see that no matter how differently we looked, we were all people. Everyone had the same needs: to eat, to be a part of something, to be loved and to have responsibilities. Certainly, it is understandable that humans don't trust what they don't know. However, in a world growing ever smaller, it seems hard to fathom how someone could dislike another for something as insignificant as skin color, disabling condition, religion or other dividers. We are all creatures trying to make the best with who and what we are. Then I thought back to the day Tom drew me the picture. I was doing the same thing those who judged Margaret and Martin were doing. I judged Tom on appearance. I had to forgive myself and the rest of humanity for such a shortcoming and hope that the more we learned and understood about each other, the quicker we'll get past racism and pity. It was at that moment I became an educator, in one way or another, for the rest of my life.

"Oh well," Martin concluded. "What can you do?"

"Love her as much as you can?"

Martin smiled, "Precisely. Will you continue to walk with us after dinner?"

"Yes, but don't be shocked when, on the last day, she gets into my Dad's car and goes home with me."

"I'll brace myself for that possibility."

At the end of camp that summer, we had this bizarre Greco-Roman toga party the last night at the chow hall. I was informed by Martin that Doug Waters, who made it possible to be at the camp but whom I had seen only once, when he tossed me and an inner tube into the pool, had decided I would sit at the head table and play the role of son to the emperor. They found me a nice white sheet and I sat with the emperor, who was the head male counselor, and the empress, who was the head female counselor. Some of the counselors were on the wrestling teams of their various colleges, and for our after-dinner entertainment, they wrestled in a series of matches. At the end of each match, we royals at the table gave thumbs up or down to determine whether the loser would live or die. I was surprised when Doug turned out to be one of the wrestlers. His opponent was about the same size. The other wore no prosthetics. Doug fought gallantly until his opponent took out a fake knife and "amputated" Doug's leg. Doug looked up to the table. The emperor immediately gave him thumbs down. The queen raised her hand, and I quickly whispered to her that Doug had made it possible for me to be there. She gave thumbs up! There was a tie now, and I was positioned to break it. I held my hand up and gave a thumbs up!

My parents were there the next day to pick me up, as scheduled. Martin walked me to the car and noticed I didn't look very happy. We never talked about my home life. I doubt I'd have been able if I were asked about it. When we arrived, Martin shook hands with my parents and told them what a good camper I was. Tom came by to see me off, and I showed him I had his drawing. We promised we'd keep in touch and see each other next year. We failed on both counts. I walked to the car door and looked up to see Margaret. She came running to me, called me her "little walker" and gave me a kiss on the cheek. As we pulled away in the car, my window was rolled down. I could see Martin with a hand on Tom's shoulder and an arm around Margaret. She was singing, "It's Too Late." To this day, I cry when I hear that song. That was the last time I'd see any of the three

# CHAPTER SEVENTEEN
# Easter Seals Camp, Part 2

If I had any questions about the potential of the human spirit if that human had a physical difference, it was quickly addressed during my second stay at Easter Seals Camp. My counselor was a man named Gene, who despite paralyzed legs was the strongest and fastest man I ever met. Gene wore braces on his legs that apparently allowed him to stand with his knees locked straight. He also used metal crutches with the forward-facing handles and the "C"-shaped band that partially surrounded the forearm. He was a very muscular man who was clearly no stranger to gyms. Often campers would challenge him to a race around the camp's circle. Gene would always give them a generous lead, then – by swinging his body forward and landing on his feet, which were far out in front of him, swinging the rest of the body past his feet, then putting his crutches in front of him – swing forward again. He was lightning fast and in two or three big strides could catch his opponent. When he first started being challenged, he would go as fast as possible and beat his challengers by at least half a lap. It didn't take long for him to begin to regret always winning, and even though he always did, he didn't continue beating them by such a huge margin. He told me one day he could see their sad faces and he realized that he was discouraging them from running. So he would hold back. He would do it in a way that they knew he was holding back. Sometimes, he'd turn around and "check" on them. Sometimes, he'd pretend to be reading a newspaper until the opponent passed him, and then he'd catch and pass them. The one thing he didn't do is let them win. "Letting someone win is lying," he often said. "If they can beat me, let them, but if I hold back, and tease them or pretend to read while they're running, they'll remember this is all for fun. They don't need to be humiliated by a loss and not falsely rewarded for a hollow victory."

One of the other counselors, near the end of the stay, and Gene got into an argument one day. We never heard the reason for the argument, but the other counselor, Andy, told Gene he always won his races but look at his opponents. Gene clearly got angry about this.

"Let's race then! You have two working legs. Let's see you beat me!"

The word of this challenge crossed the camp in seconds. We gathered right outside our cabin, and the whole camp came to watch. People were sitting on the lawn of our cabin, on the porch and on the hill on the other side. Wheelchair users were lined up on the cabin side of the street. The last wheelchair to the right of the cabin was designated as the finish line. The girl in the chair and another counselor held the ribbon they found somewhere for the actual finish line. The runners were to start on the other side of the ribbon. When the racers took their positions, the head resident came out to officiate the race. He held his hand in the air like a flag, and waved downward with a loud "Go!" Andy took a quick lead. Gene was moving more slowly than usual. This made no sense to me. Gene was always a quick starter. They ran around the curve in the circle and went out of sight. When they reappeared on the left, they had a little less than a quarter of the loop to run. Gene was still behind!

Suddenly Gene kicked into gear. Instead of just his usual style of running, he now was tossing himself forward as he swung his legs forward. It looked unstable and I'm sure we all worried he'd fall, but he gained ground quickly and passed Andy, who slowed as Gene crossed the finish and turned to see Andy arrive. Gene turned a little too quickly. Lost his balance and fell. Andy walked over and shouted over the commotion, "You won, but it killed you to do it."

"No, I just thought I'd get in a little nap while you were finishing up."

That night, as we were getting ready for bed, Gene came in to talk with us. One of the campers shouted, "Way to go, Gene!" He pulled up a chair and sat among us.

"Boys, you win a few, and you lose a few. That's not the important thing. When someone like Andy – and Andy is my friend – but when someone calls you out like that you have a decision to make. You can sit, think about your disability and let it determine what you do, or you can stand up, roll up, whatever you do and be a man or woman first. Andy is healthy. He takes care of his body. Good for him. But if he challenges me, I let nothing get in my way. I answer the challenge. Win or lose."

In the summer of 1973, I was at camp for the next to the last time. I was beginning to feel like the elder of the camp because I was now a teenager and had been here more frequently than the rest of these young ones. A tradition the camp had continued each year I attended was that at lunch, a "Camper of the Day" was selected. I thought it a bit sad that after three years as a camper, I had never been selected. I complained to a fellow camper about this, and apparently, he repeated my complaint because the next day, magically, I was "Camper of the Day." I walked up front and was given a badge of the Easter Seals Society to wear for the day. I was told I'd get a surprise the last day the recognitions were given, but I had no idea what that might be.

It was fun living as a camp celeb for a day. "Hey, Walt! Congratulations, buddy!" and "Nice badge!" were the usual greetings. I thanked them, and we moved on. On the next to the last day of camp, the head counselor stopped me as I was beginning my trek to the chow hall for breakfast. "Not so fast, Mr. Camper of the Day. You and your other awarded colleagues are being treated to a day on the houseboat today."

"Houseboat? Who has a houseboat?"

"The camp has one; it was given to us by a donor. You and the other CODs and a couple of counselors who haven't made me mad yet will have a day on the lake, with a secret stop, I understand. You are to report ASAP to the boat dock, where you will have a boxed breakfast, a picnic lunch, a special stop, then back at camp for evening chow."

I reported to the dock. A counselor we called "Captain Fred" was our cruise director for the day. There were eight campers of the day, four girls and four boys, and a corresponding counselor for each gender. I noticed the campers who were selected were matched by disability: There were two campers with leg prosthetics, two wheelchair users, two blind campers and two campers with intellectual disabilities. I mentioned this observation to the female counselor named Stacy, a tough-as-nails, no-panic kind of brunette who clearly lived her life without skimping on pleasures like good food. I have always thought women who enjoy their lives are by their very nature more attractive than skinny women who are afraid to eat. That is not to say only thick-bodied women are attractive. I know some who are fierce about eating healthily and are strong in their thinness.

Stacy smiled, "You got us, Professor." She told me later she called me that because I was smart and wore glasses. It was a moniker that would stick with me until I stopped attending camp. "It is fairer to the campers to try to have every type of disability represented as Campers of the Day. We have a few students who are deaf who aren't represented at this camp, but we usually include them. Deaf kids often consider themselves different from the rest because they don't usually like to be considered disabled, so there are other camps for them."

The boat started, backed out of the dock and turned to go out into the main part of the lake. I asked permission to see the cabin. Captain Fred motioned me to come, and I entered the cabin and approached the console. He explained to me that this was "a 1969 River Queen 40 Houseboat with 318 dual Chrysler engines. She's 40' x 12' with three steps down to the head. She has a fully stocked kitchen and two futons. A family of four could live on this beauty!"

"How does she handle?" I tried to sound like I knew what I was talking about. Captain Fred stood from his seat and offered me a chance to steer. I sat in the chair and held the wheel as if I were expecting gale-force winds. He let me make a couple of turns, and it was fun to throttle up and kick the front of the boat up as she gained speed. When it was time to give the wheel back, I did so reluctantly. When I turned from bow to stern, I saw those in chairs had flipped them over and the campers in wheelchairs were turned to the stern. They were trying to make it look like the whiplash I caused by speeding up the boat either turned or flipped them over! We had a good laugh, and I turned the wheelchairs back around and locked them as the others returned their seats to their places. Oddly, we were then given BB guns. We were told they were loaded, and we could feel free to shoot at fish, birds, snakes or any other wildlife we encountered. We had all had rifle training on the shooting range, but giving a group of kids BB guns to shoot without restrictions seemed very dangerous. Then, I aimed my gun at the water very near the boat and pulled the trigger. There was a firing shot, but nothing hit the water. The guns were empty. I looked over at the male counselor, Bobby, and he put a finger over his lips and shushed me. We all began shooting snakes and birds, and either we were the worst shots this side of the Rio Grande or our guns were unloaded, as I had already discovered, but no one else seemed to notice. We were just a bunch of wild kids shooting our way across the lake.

Around 10 a.m., Captain Fred found a good spot to drop anchor very close to a rocky beach. We got off the boat, and Stacy and Bobby unloaded fishing gear, tackle and picnic baskets. Stacy unrolled a couple of blankets, and the girl campers helped her set up a place for everyone to sit and to eat lunch later in the day. Bobby leaned fishing poles against a tree and took bait and applied it to hooks. Worms were the bait of the day, and the guys couldn't resist watching them get impaled on the hooks.

There are many fine people in the world who love to fish, and I am glad they do. I love to eat fish, but I don't like catching them. Maybe it was because my dad loved to fish, and every time he took us out he would get angry and start shouting and threatening to throw us overboard, knowing none of us could swim. I always hated being trapped in that small fishing boat surrounded by a great expanse of water with shores on both sides, and there I was, trapped on a floating box: trapped, caught, convicted, punished and had nowhere in the world I could go.

We were lined up on the beach and allowed to pick our pole. I chose a blue one because it was my favorite color. Bobby laughed and told me the color wouldn't be helpful in catching a fish. I told him if I was to stand pointlessly on a riverbank doing very little, I might as well have my favorite color in front of me. The rest chuckled. Bobby was annoyed; a lifelong smartass was awakened.

After an hour or so, we were all hot and bored, so the decision was made to go swimming. I didn't want to swim, but I was glad they did to break the monotony. My prosthetics can't be used in the water, and the idea of taking them off and crawling across a pebbled beach to the water did not sound appealing. So the others splashed into the water, and I re-boarded the houseboat and sat under the canopy drinking a refreshing beverage.

One of the boys on the trip was named Leonard, nicknamed Lennie, and Lennie was intellectually challenged, although such a polite term did not exist at the time. The wheelchair-using campers were being assisted by Bobby and Stacy, and Captain Jack was entertaining the others, but Lennie seemed to be slowly wandering away from the group. I decided I'd better keep an eye on him. Like me, Lennie wasn't a swimmer. He walked along the bottom, bouncing step by step, enjoying the buoyancy.

Bobby saw Lennie wandering out too deep, and, carrying another boy, he went to get him. When he reached Lennie, he grabbed Lennie's upper arm and pulled him back. Lennie began to shout and cry and told Bobby to leave him alone. Bobby explained, "You were wandering too far off, Lennie. I didn't want you to get hurt." Lennie continued to cry. Then, possibly to distract him, Bobby whispered to the boy he was carrying, and the two of them began splashing Lennie. Lennie's hair and face were quickly soaked, and his crying began to change. It was no longer the loud shouting that intends to notify the world you want something to stop. It became the desperate cry of someone who is trapped, scared and angry. I knew the sound. It was familiar to my ears, and throat. I stood and began to pace around the boat as they splashed and splashed. I began muttering to myself that they needed to stop, but they couldn't hear me, and wouldn't if they could have. I watched as Lennie shouted and shouted. He was reaching for something. Was he reaching to push them away, reaching for a hand to grab ahold of him and pull him out of this, or was he reaching through the slats in the barn door to unlock the door and let him out? I was pacing in a figure eight, around and around, sweating, tears and sweat mingled mid-cheek to form a type of spiritual blood, and I felt the bond between me and Lennie. I couldn't breathe. I was trapped in that stable cell again; water was ceaselessly being splashed on me and I couldn't breathe. "Stop splashing him! Please let me out! I didn't mean to cry!!!!" I had fallen to my knees and was crying. I heard the words I shouted but hadn't yet realized I had shouted them. Everyone was now perfectly quiet. My arms were resting on the top rail, and I was crying. Captain Fred and Stacy got out of the water, sat a girl camper in her wheelchair and got on board. They didn't kneel or touch me. Maybe they were going to contain me if I exploded again. Lennie was the first to break the silence. "Professor, you OK?"

"Yeah, Lennie. You?"

"I don't like it when they splash me."

"Clearly, I don't either." Bobby didn't make eye contact with me. Everyone got out of the water, I was helped off the boat, and we opened the baskets and had sandwiches, chips, and milk or water for lunch. There was a silence that engulfed the group while we ate. While eating, I looked out over the water to see if the black cloud I had exorcised was floating away. It must have dispersed because I saw it nowhere. I would later realize I had reabsorbed it; it would come out from time to time for years to come.

We finished lunch, and Bobby announced we were ready for our special treat. There was a cave a short walk up the hill from where we sat. The baskets were put back onboard the boat, and we passed into the trees and saw a well-worn path leading to a gentle uphill climb. It was an easy path even for the wheelchairs, by design of course. We arrived in minutes. The mouth of the cave wasn't a yawn as much as it was an open-mouthed frown. The adults had to bow to enter. Inside there was a stream flowing along the floor, forcing me to walk with my back or side against an uneven, wet cave wall. We walked until there was a split in the walkway. Captain Fred and I decided we'd go to the left. The rest were going right. Captain Fred had a flashlight, which we now needed. We walked a while, and then he asked if I were scared. "Why should I be? All three of you have been here many times."

Captain Fred smiled. "How did you know?"

"The worn trail was a dead giveaway. Besides, you wouldn't bring a bunch of kids to a cave you'd never seen, then split up."

"Not much gets past you, does it boy?" The Captain smiled. "Maybe you'd like to talk about what happened earlier while everyone was swimming, except you."

"I didn't like seeing Lennie get picked on. He kept shouting 'No!' and no one seemed to care."

"I'm sure that's true. But you were somewhere else. You were here and somewhere in your head. Want to tell me what's going on?"

Captain Fred seemed to be a nice man. I wanted to talk with him and tell him everything. I wanted to discuss the relationship I had with my parents, especially with my dad, and see if he could shed some light on it. I didn't because I didn't have the words. Do all dads do what mine has done? Do they all hit, abandon or lock away their sons? I was afraid that the other dads don't do this. If they do, then dads are just bastards that we all have to survive. If only my dad does this, then maybe I am beaten and locked away because something is wrong with me. I was afraid to admit something might be wrong with me, so I told him nothing.

I turned 13 a few days before my last year at Easter Seals Camp, and I was beginning to feel like I was a staff member. Everyone called me Professor now, and I looked a little like one with my round body and face, shortly cropped hair, and the boy version of cat's-eyeglasses. I was a horror show on prosthetics, but I was a teenager now, and that made all the difference.

My counselor that last year, Bill, was a psychology major at Vanderbilt. His area of study was children with Down syndrome. He had several kids with DS assigned to him, and he had a handheld recorder that he would carry with him throughout the day. He constantly recorded observations he made about them throughout the day. He assured me the kids were getting to do the same things other kids did, he was only recording them doing their various activities. Their parents signed a waiver for their kids to be a part of Bill's study, and they attended camp at a lower cost than the other campers.

One night at dinner, Bill and I were discussing Roger, one of the kids with DS. Roger was sitting beside Bill, and Bill was helping Roger with his meal, but Roger seemed completely unaware that we were discussing him. "Their self-awareness has limits," Bill explained. "For example, Roger, did you know you have Down syndrome?"

Roger ate his meal, smiling, not answering the question or even recognizing it was asked. We finished the meal and walked back to the cabin. There was no special event that evening, so I found myself without anything to do. I started thinking about my first year, about Tom, Martin and Margaret, and I decided to walk around the camp circle. I walked counterclockwise around the camp. As I passed the girls' cabins the ears of my memory picked up the faint sounds of the song "It's Too Late" rustling through the leaves above me. The tree limbs blew in the breeze and caused their shadows to dance slowly to the tune until I could vaguely discern the image of a ghostly Margaret leaning on Martin's shoulder. I continued around until I was in front of the ramp leading to the boat dock. At first glance, I would have sworn I saw Tom in shadows drawing the boat dock, pencil in his mouth. My three years at this camp had given me many gifts, but the most important was the feeling of being a part of a family. I had no idea where they went, but wherever they were in the universe, I sent them thoughts of love and gratitude.

That night, after lights out, I was lying on my side slowly beginning to fall asleep, when I suddenly felt a depression on the mattress behind me. I could hear heavy breathing and slurping behind me. I was frozen stiff, afraid that movement would prove unwise. The breathing continued, slowly, rhythmically. I considered screaming, or jumping up and calling for help, but what if the sound was coming from further away than I thought, and I was under no threat. So I listened as closely as I could. Every now and again, I would hear short vocalizations in the breathing, slight moans, or voiced sounds mixed with sighs, and I realized it was Roger I heard. I gathered my nerve and asked, "Roger, is that you?"

"Yes," he answered, "it's me."

"I'm going to roll over, OK?" I didn't wait for permission. I turned and found him sitting, leaning over me, mouth agape. "What do you want, Roger?"

"Toothpaste!" He said this almost loudly enough to wake the others. I noticed he had toothpaste on his lips. He looked and smelled like he had eaten toothpaste. "Why do you want it?"

"I like the taste!" He confirmed my suspicion. He had been going up the side of the room, looking into each camper's storage shelves for toothpaste and eating what he found. Why he chose to sit on my bunk and breathe into my ear was a mystery, but he didn't seem very threatening.

I wasn't sure it was a good idea for Roger to eat several tubes of toothpaste, so I told him I'd have to ask Bill if it's OK. He began to pace around nervously as I slipped past him and went to the counselors' room and awoke Bill. He came into the big room and saw Roger sitting on my bed, rocking back and forth and whimpering quietly to himself. Bill sat beside him and put his arm around Roger's shoulder. "How are you doing, buddy?" he asked.

"I'm fine," he assured Bill.

"Why are you eating toothpaste?"

"I like the way it's soft in my mouth, and it's cool and tingly."

"Have you ever tried chewing gum?"

"My mom won't let me have it because I swallow it," Roger replied, looking very sad about this.

"By morning, your tummy may be quite upset by the toothpaste, too. I think you need to stop now, what do you think?"

"OK, I stop. You're not mad at me, are you, Bill?" Roger put his head on Bill's shoulder.

"How could I ever be mad at you?" Bill responded as he gently put his arm around Roger.

I thought about this camp many times after I stopped attending. I have searched for it on the computer and have often wondered whatever happened to the people I encountered there. I don't know why "goodbyes" are often permanent in life but "hellos" seldom are. What did remain of that camp lived on in my heart. I understood that without feet, I could stand as a man; without hands I could hold others and mold a future; with the knowledge that there are others like me somewhere in the world – standing, holding, living – we could support each other wherever we were with a web of human connectedness woven by the understanding that we are differently the same. When I left Easter Seals Camp, I walked with my head up. Frank Nelson would have only a couple more chances to hurt me, and then that era of our relationship would be over.

# CHAPTER EIGHTEEN

# Teachers

In the sixth grade, for a reason unknown to me, we were required to run around and around the gym in P.E. class. We did this for the entire class period. We did it every day. Our "teacher," Coach whatever, stood in the middle of the gym, twirling his whistle around his index finger more frequently than we ran laps, and possibly for the same reason. One day, while chasing my backside, I noticed I was having a technical problem. Underneath my prosthetic legs, I wore these thick 5-ply wool socks over my biological legs. As I ran or exercised, my socks would become sweaty, and as the prosthetic pistoned up and down on my leg, my socks sometimes wrinkled and slid partially down the leg. This would create a very large fold of fabric underneath my leg, and that would, over time, start cutting into my skin. Once it starts, taking off the prosthetic is only a temporary solution, but it is better than continuing to walk on it. Continuing would result in a blister or a break in the skin; both are painful for several days. I could feel that the sock was very sweaty and slipping into the bottom, so I asked Coach if I could stop and readjust. He said, "No," so I tried to explain what would happen if I didn't, and he said, "It's about time we stopped coddling you and require you to grow up like everybody else!" I was to continue until he told us to stop. I could feel the fold forming, and soon the familiar sting of blistering skin began. I limped back over to him to ask again, but he pointed to the circle of students and wouldn't even listen. As I was slowly making my last circle around the gym, I could feel real damage being done, so I walked to the bleachers without asking. As soon as I sat, the bell rang. The coach shouted that if I were going to be a crybaby, I had to leave his gym and cry elsewhere. I stood and limped on my other leg, and I somehow made to my social studies class. I collapsed into my desk, removed the prosthetic, and revealed a sweaty sock with a small, bloody stain at the bottom. My teacher, Mrs. Warner, wanted to know what had happened. When I explained, she stood and marched from the room, shouting, "We'll see about this!"

My classmates and I could hear her stomping all the way to the gym where she entered, shouting, "Do you know what you did to that boy?" If he ever responded, we couldn't hear him. "He just took his shoe and sock off in my classroom, and that boy's leg is bleeding! And why, so he can run endless, meaningless circles around you while you spin your little whistle? I hope his parents sue you, the school, the superintendent and the school board until you stop hurting kids!" Seconds later, she was back in the room. We all looked away like we didn't just hear every word she said. "Do you need a nurse? Would you like to talk with the principal?" I assured her I needed neither of them.

That evening, as my family sat down for dinner, Dad informed me that Mrs. Warner had called. He asked that I explain what had happened. I told him briefly, and he seemed to anger as my story progressed. Upon my conclusion, he stated, "It seems to me that Coach is just trying to make a man out of you! Is that what they taught you at that camp?" Since I returned from the camp this past summer, Dad has acted like I'm somehow a threat to him. I am.

"No, that's not what they taught me. They taught me to stand up for myself when something is going wrong. I wasn't asking Coach to let me skip the exercise, I was just …"

Since when did you start lecturing me in my own home?" Frank was getting angrier.

"I'm not trying to lecture you, I'm just ..."

"How about you shut up and listen. I didn't raise kids who'll lie around and complain. We are workers. You're going to work, and I don't care what fingers and toes you're missing. Do you understand?"

I didn't really, but I'd have never admitted that. He was standing, pacing now. He was making a plan that I would not like. "I tell you what. I started mowing the lawn before dinner. I finished the hill in the back. The sides and front still need mowing. Why don't you finish those before dark?"

"That will take me three hours. I have homework to do, and my leg is still very sore from P.E. today. Dad, can't I finish mowing this weekend?"

"Since you aren't feeling well, I'll help you get outside." He circled around behind me before I could stand and picked me up out of my chair. He led me by the collar and waist of my pants amid the quiet protestations of Mom, Beth and Frankie. None of them dared speak too loudly, or they'd go with me. Out on the lawn, Dad started the mower for me, looked at his watch, and said, "Three hours," and he smiled walking back into the house. Dad liked the grass mowed by doing each pass in opposite directions, so the lawn looked striped when finished. My first decision was to ignore that, divide the lawn into sections and mow in spiraling smaller and smaller circles, so I would have some shot at finishing on time.

The thing that saved me was that Mom had changed my socks when I got home. Once they began wrinkling, as they did in class, they would continue until they were washed. My leg still bled again, but I pushed through until I finished. I had no idea how long it took and didn't care. I killed the mower, returned it to the shed, and went into the house. Dad was in the bathroom, so I went to my room and shut my door. The only air conditioner we had was a window unit that was kept in my room. It couldn't be in any other room because my room and my parents' room were side by side at the back of the house. My parents didn't put it in their room because they might want to shut the door for privacy. The other rooms would not allow air to flow out to the rest of the house, so since I didn't need privacy, the air unit was mine. I turned the vents to blow toward my bed and lay down dropping off to sleep. When Dad came out of the bathroom, the house seemed warmer. He looked toward my room, and he saw the door was closed. Mom was walking down the hallway, and he stopped her and asked how long I'd been inside. "Ten minutes maybe," she guessed. He crossed to the den window where he could see the lawn was mowed.

Dad walked quickly to my room, opened the door and grabbed my shirt and belt. I was startled awake; it had been a while since my surgeries, and I had grown unaccustomed to being awakened this way. Dad picked me up and tossed me against the wall. He picked me up again, threw me again, and each time gravity dribbled me onto my bed. This continued, and I did everything in my power not to cry, shout or scream. I understood now, those reactions just fed him. After the fourth toss, I could feel he was weakening. He soon stopped and stood me on my feet. My face must have been the color of blood, but I did not cry.

"From now on, always do what you're told. If a teacher wants you to run, run. If I want you to mow, mow! There is no back talk in this house. Do you hear me?" The question was asked in an ever-rising voce, like a drill instructor would ask it.

"I understand."

"You aren't at camp anymore. I expect obedience, respect and hard work out of you. Got that?"

I wanted so badly to answer, "Sir, yes, sir!" but I knew better. "Yes, sir."

He told me to leave the air vents aimed toward the door and to leave the door open, and with that, I was dismissed for the night.

The next morning, Mrs. Warner had me paged to the office. I was led into the principal's office. Mrs. Warner and the principal both wanted to know what my parents' reactions were to my leg.

"Dad was mad."

"Well, son, he had a right to be," my principal began to explain. "I'll call your parents today and see if they'd like to come in and see me, and maybe they could have a word with Coach.

"I don't think that's necessary."

"Why not?" he asked.

"Dad's not mad at Coach. He's mad at me. He made me mow the lawn to remind me not to refuse to obey orders." The principal looked at Mrs. Warner with a look that seemed to relay relief that there would be no legal repercussions in this matter and sorrow that Dad punished me because Coach was an asshole. He assured me that I was relieved of gym duty for the rest of the school year. He told me that my science teacher, Mr.

Blalock, needed a teacher's aide, and if I wanted, I could do that instead. They explained that I would grade papers, put things away and set up for classes. It sounded good to me.

The principal seemed to want to wrap this discussion up with a bow. He said, "You know you didn't deserve to be punished because of what happened in gym class yesterday. I don't know why your dad wanted you to mow the lawn after what happened, but if it was for a punishment, you did nothing wrong. Making you mow on an injured leg solved nothing."

"And yet, I'm being moved out of gym class, and Coach gets to stay. Do you think he'll feel punished when I don't show up today?"

I was sent to Mr. Blalock's class. The principal's sympathy was depleted.

"Let's try an experiment, Mr. Nelson." Mr. Blalock always called students by their last names. "Let's learn about the speed of light." Ironically, he turned off the lights for this experiment. He had me sit on the side of the room. He took his place at the front of the room, a flashlight in his hands. "Now, when I turn on the flashlight, I want you to try and follow the beam of light to the back wall. Think you can do it?"

"Yes, sir!" I was excited to try. Mr. Blalock smiled.

"Boy, light travels at 186,000 miles per second. According to NASA, light can travel around the equator 7.5 times in one second, and your eyes can follow it to the wall?"

"I'll try my best." Mr. Blalock liked the enthusiasm.

"Here we go!" Blalock turned on the light, as I spun my head toward the back of the room as quickly as I could.

"Could you see the beam of light moving?"

"Yes, I could!"

"Boy, you can't turn your head that fast. Try again." We tried again. I could see it moving. Mr. Blalock walked over to me, put his hand on top of my head and pretended to hit me. "Gonna knock some sense into you, boy." It was funny. We both laughed. We tried a third time. I still saw it, so Mr. Blalock pulled up a chair and sat facing me.

"I'll tell you, Mr. Nelson, why I like you. You don't back down. I can tell you what NASA says, pop you in the head and try multiple times, but you stick to it. You not only stick to your story, in your imagination, I believe you really do see that light traveling across the room. You have a mind, Mr. Nelson, and it's hard to find a good one. Your math scores suggest a future in science might not be for you, but with your intellect and imagination, there will be very few doors closed to you. I think you and I should spend this time exploring that imagination of yours. How do you feel about that?"

How was I supposed to feel? A teacher just found a redeeming quality in me.

Each day working as Mr. Blalock's aide was enjoyable. Sometimes we did grade papers. Sometimes we set up labs for the classes to do. Sometimes we tried labs to preview how they'd work. Usually though, Mr. Blalock would bring pictures to school. He would show them to me, and I would make up stories about who they were and what they were doing. Most of his pictures were of him and others while he was stationed in Hawaii during the Korean War. I asked him if he ever went to Korea, and he said he did but we wouldn't be looking at those pictures here. I asked him why not, and he assured me there were some pictures I didn't need to see.

Mr. Blalock was one of those teachers who left an imprint on my soul, as most good teachers do. He taught me that no one could tell me what I could or could not perceive, and he taught me that the mind, if engaged fully, could never be imprisoned.

My school was divided into two parts: The elementary school contained first through sixth grades; the high school contained seventh through 12th grades. The year before I entered high school, there had been a racially motivated fight that swept across the campus. The police were called to restore order; one teacher's arm was broken; and several students were hospitalized. Over the summer, my principal from elementary was placed in command of the high school, and the first black vice principal that area had ever known was brought in. The two worked well together. They spent time encouraging team spirit, opening activities to all students, and teaching us to be proud of ourselves and our school.

It was perhaps this new awareness of how the unique individual can contribute to the beauty of the whole that led Mrs. Chamberlain to notice my oddly shaped self as I entered her classroom the first day. She noticed a limp and the lack of right hand and three fingers on the left and decided immediately to call and talk with my mom. After school that day, she called and asked my mom what she should do to ensure the other kids did not run off and leave me academically.

My mom laughed and said, "That's not your problem, Mrs. Chamberlain."

"What do you mean?"

"You will need to figure out how to keep Walt from leaving the other kids."

The next day, Mrs. Chamberlain told the other teachers this story. I believe this may have raised expectations of my abilities, and as I moved from class to class I was usually greeted with a sense of curiosity instead of the sense of worry or annoyance I seemed to inspire in elementary classes.

My Achilles' heel in high school and in life was mathematics. I am right-brain dominant with a love of the arts, music and the written word. I am left-brained enough to admire philosophy and logical thinking, but I prefer to consider how philosophy feels rather than understand its complexities, and I love the structure and order of logical thought, but rather than persuading with my razor-sharp proofs, I am limited to weaving emotional stories that tug on the heartstrings.

When I, the romantic poet, entered the class of the basketball-coaching, algebra-teaching burnout, the scene was set for tragedy. Every day, the coach would enter the classroom dribbling a ball. He would sit on top of his desk and regale us with heroic stories of amazing athletes snatching balls mid-air and charging to a netted Valhalla. After the stories, he would collect homework, which he would briefly review, and give us a quiz. The following day, we would get the quizzes back, graded, and in order of the worst quiz to the best. I always got mine first with either an "F" or "D" emblazoned on top. The look in his eyes was a mixture of pity and contempt, which was fair because my look back was pure contempt. One day, at the end of class, an announcement interrupted my boredom. The ballots for student council had been counted and I had been elected representative for my class. Not to miss out on making a poignant pedagogical point, Coach Dumbass said, "If Mr. Nelson spent less time trying to be popular and more time on his studies, he might have better grades in this class."

Not one to back down from a fight, I responded, "If you spent less time dribbling balls and more time actually teaching algebra, I might have better grades in this class." I was sent to the principal for being a smartass. The principal agreed with both of our assessments.

My senior year, I was placed in the classroom of a giant. Mrs. Farmer stood by the door and greeted us every day as we entered with, "Come in, seniors," reminding us we had earned enough status to be in her class. That was no guarantee we would get out of it, though. Her class was amphitheater style, and Mrs. Farmer would walk those steps every day and perch herself on the edge of her desk as our queen. Mrs. Farmer was thin and had a frail look about her, but one would underestimate her to one's own peril. She was in command. She was smarter than we were, and if we wanted to graduate, she was the gatekeeper who decided our fate.

Mrs. Farmer had a practice she used every time we wrote papers. As she read them, she would assign an "F" to our papers if we made a mistake in grammar that she had already taught us. If we disagreed with her assessment, we were invited to stand behind her seldom-used lectern and make our case. If we could prove our point, we would get an "A," and if we couldn't there was no harm done. We didn't know what this process was like because Mrs. Farmer was so scary, no one ever challenged her.

One day, all that changed. I received an "F." I couldn't believe my eyes; I love grammar and was the sentence-diagramming champion of my school. Frantically, I flipped through the pages until I found the offending error. I had used the indefinite pronoun "none" as the subject of a sentence coupled with a plural verb. The antecedent of the pronoun was "students" and followed as an object of the preposition after "none." Certainly, Mrs. Farmer knew this was correct. I hadn't made an error! I glanced at her quickly and caught her watching me. She looked away without a change in facial expression, but I believe I understood. She wanted me to contest the grade, so others could see it was possible. She was teaching us a lesson about standing up for ourselves.

"Yes, Mr. Nelson?" she asked in response to my raised hand.

"I believe you made an error on my paper," I said, my heart racing. Would my dad be furious? Will she lose her respect for me?

"Come to the lectern, if you wish, Mr. Nelson. I'm sure we are all anxious to hear your case." Every eye in the classroom was on me, and I could almost hear their thoughts. They were trying to tell me telepathically that Mrs. Farmer didn't make mistakes. I was putting my grade, my chances at graduating and my health in danger all at once. I even thought I heard the whistling song one hears in a duel scene in a spaghetti western as I rounded the lectern.

Armed with my grammar book and paper, I asked the congregation to turn to the chapter on pronouns. We read the rules about indefinite ones, and about how some were either singular or plural depending upon their antecedent. I then looked at Mrs. Farmer, smiled and respectfully rested my case.

She quickly walked to the lectern with a smile on her face. She explained to the class that I was right. They applauded, weakly. Audiences usually prefer to hang the guilty rather than celebrate the innocent. Mrs. Farmer explained that for the first half of her career, her students referred to her as the Queen of Grammar, and it was her pleasure to now name me the King of Grammar! Despite the very light applause, I claimed the moniker until about halfway through my teaching career. By that point, students didn't believe teachers were the kings or queens of anything.

Mrs. Farmer and all my other teachers had taught me to stand up for myself and for what's right when I needed to do so. In June 1978, I graduated.

# CHAPTER NINETEEN
## Revolution

I lived with my parents for a year after graduation. Many great things happened during that year, but I was never allowed to forget in whose home I lived or under whose rules I served. One summer night, a group of my friends called and invited me to go out and have some fun. I enthusiastically agreed, and they offered to come by my house and pick me up. I began to get ready when the phone rang again. It was Dad. He never used a greeting with me over the phone. "My truck won't start," he began. "When your mom gets home, have her call me and come pick me up."

I remembered my dad's message as my friends pulled up the driveway, so I asked Beth to tell Mom his message. She promised she would, and out the door I fled looking for adventure. A few minutes later, Beth's friends came to get her. She left without a note, ensuring I would find an adventure, whether I wanted it or not.

I came in around 12:30 and Dad was waiting by the door. "What did I tell you to do?" I could see how the anger had built up in his eyes.

"You told me to have Mom call because your truck wouldn't start, but I went out with my friends, so I asked Beth …"

"Leave Beth out of this. I didn't ask anything of Beth. I told you to tell your mom, and you ran out without a thought and left me stranded."

"Did you ask Beth …?"

"Turns out she has friends, too, but that takes me back to the point that I didn't ask anything of her. I asked it of you."

"When Mom got home and saw no one near, didn't she call …?"

"We are all to blame but you, aren't we?"

"No, Dad. I didn't do what you told me to do. I'm sorry."

"Too bad that won't cut it."

"What do you mean?" I knew exactly what that meant. I had seen that angry face many times.

"Go to your room and bend over the bed," he ordered as he took off his belt.

"Come on, Dad! I'm 18 years old. I start college in a few weeks. Can't we work this out?"

"I told you what to do. You didn't do it. You were a big man saying no. I'm the big man saying, 'Yes!!!' Now, go to your room and bend over or I'll break your jaw."

Something happened to me on that walk down the hallway toward my room. I heard the fragile shell of my childhood crack and crumble. I could no longer stand, like a wet, cold, newborn chick afraid of Dad's grownup power. My feathers were dry, and I could feed myself. It was time to break the bonds, jump from the nest and land where I land.

I entered the room and leaned over my bed. Dad wound the belt several circles around his hand leaving enough left over to use as a whip. He brought it down on my butt as hard as he could. He kept swinging and swinging, until I had a revelation. I remembered the night I was left out in the snow. My resolve not to cry came back, and I kept my old pledge. I soon realized that I wasn't being brave; he really wasn't hurting me. Soon, he tired and stopped. He looked around to my face and asked if I had had enough. It was time for the kill.

"Why? Is that all you've got?" I responded with a smile. His face contorted unrecognizably as he pushed me over and started thrashing me again. He was angrier and swinging harder, but his energy was waning.

116

He stopped, and I stood again. No more smart-aleck words. This time, I pushed him hard against the wall. I pinned him there with my arms, while he looked startled into my eyes.

"You are never to touch me again without my permission for the rest of your life. If you do, I will break your arm off and beat you senseless with it. I am a grown man, and I demand you treat me like one. Do you understand me?"

He spun out from my hold and walked to the doorway of the room. There, he turned back. There was no expression on his face; the anger was gone. "It's about time" was all he said. We never spoke of it again. He also never hit me again.

I finished my first year at Austin Peay State University. It was a good year. I took an honors English series that I loved, got elected to the student senate, and became active in the drama department. That winter still found my dad and me arguing over what I may and may not do. So I filled out applications and secured a student loan, and that summer I was on a bus headed for a University in Tennessee. My parents weren't paying. This was my risk, to succeed or fail. I was a free man and had no intension of failing.

CHAPTER TWENTY

# Campus Life

I took a bus to Knoxville for my orientation weekend to the campus. I had never taken a bus by myself, and I had never moved away from home. So, as I reached up and ran my thumb across the few hairs that would eventually multiply, thicken and form for me a mustache I would keep most of my life, I thought myself quite a man. I kept hearing Paul Simon and Art Garfunkel singing about looking for America, even though I was traveling only a little over 400 miles by interstate across half of Tennessee. This was my first time in East Tennessee and as I saw those great hills in the distance growing higher and higher, I wondered if I would know a mountain when I saw one. I would not.

I was attending transfer-student orientation. It was shorter than the regular program for incoming freshmen. There was a dinner with guest speakers, and a "get acquainted" dance the first night. The next day, there was breakfast, a campus tour, meeting time with your intended college of study, a "talent" show staged by student orientation assistants. Then we escaped back to our homes. Even though I had been accepted by UT, I didn't have a dorm room yet. During our meeting time, I found the head resident of the fifth largest freshman dorm in the country and begged for a room. He told me there were no rooms left, but he could put me on a waiting list.

"How can I come here in the fall without a room?"

"That's a fair question," he reasoned, "but I can't give you what I don't have." He asked me several questions about accessibility. Many classes are located on top of a tall hill. Would I make it to class on time? I told him I would. Can I navigate the cafeterias on my own? Yes, I've been eating for years. Can I keep up with college courses? I told him about my experiences and activities at APSU. I could do this. As he ran out of questions, I assured him that I appreciated his concern. UTK had accepted me, and that must mean I had a fighting chance to graduate. He told me UT had a high new-student dropout rate, and I promised him I would not be one of them. He was flipping through pages when he told me he had a room designated as a handicapped room if I were interested. I told him I had a physical difference, not a "handicap," and wanted a regular room, with the normal UTK experience. He handed me a room form with a smile. "You will make it here, won't you?"

I finally got a room, and a roommate who enjoyed green brownies. I had communal showers, visitation three times a week, a hall mate who went from room to room, accompanied by his beautiful but terribly embarrassed girlfriend, trying to borrow a condom from a floor of guys who never had or needed them. I asked her once after her boyfriend failed to get a condom from me why she followed him around being embarrassed like that. She blinked, showing the void behind her eyes, and asked why not. He brought other girls around, too, so we could see what a "cool" guy he was. I was unimpressed.

My niche, it turned out was in student politics. There was an ad in the campus newspaper urging students who might be new to campus to get involved in the Student Government Association. Student senators were elected from geographical locations around campus, and those, along with elections for president, vice president, secretary and treasurer were held in the spring. In the fall, the way to get involved was by applying to be a member of a student services committee. They were all listed in the ad, and as a pre-law student, I was quickly attracted to the Student Rights

Committee. I called the number on the ad and got an appointment to interview with the chairman of the committee, Steven Becker.

When I walked to the interview the next day, I wondered what kind of questions Steve would ask. Would my interest in law help me? Was he looking for experience? I had some experience, but I didn't know if a big-shot committee chairman at Tennessee's flagship university would be impressed.

I arrived at the office of the Student Government Association 15 minutes early. A college girl was sitting behind the desk with the secretary nameplate on it, and I told her I was there to see Steven Becker. She congratulated me and went back to reading a paperback. I took a seat on the couch, and after 20 minutes passed, the door to the vice president's office opened. Two men exited, and one asked the secretary if a Walter Nelson had shown up. I stood declaring, "I'm here, sir. I'm Walter." He smiled at the "sir" and took me into the office. There was a desk at the back middle of the office, a couch on the left side, two guest chairs in front of the desk, and the vice president, Alex Goodman, pulled his chair to the right of the guest chairs. The chairman, Steve, sat on the couch, and I was in a guest chair. I was flanked on both sides. I was seated like this in offices many times in my professional life; it never worked. Both guys had sheets of paper in front of them with their questions. They took turns, ripped through the questions and gave me the impression that neither was listening. After completing their list, they asked if I had anything to add. I said, "Yes. When this becomes my office, I'll pay attention to the answers I'm getting." They laughed, welcomed me to the committee, ushered me out and continued to laugh at the arrogant upstart as the door closed. It became my office in two years.

The committee didn't do much until an issue was referred to us from the Student Senate. It was 1979, and America was embroiled in the Iranian hostage crisis. Fifty-two Americans had been captured when Iranian students seized control of the American Embassy in Tehran. Iranian students who were studying on American college campuses were sharing with the world what they believed were America's great sins, and students around the country, including UTK, were tired of listening. The issue came to our committee in a simple request. A note from the president said, "The Student Senate is considering taking up the matter and possibly asking the administration to limit Iranian student free speech on campus ... I'm asking this committee to see if you would recommend a restriction on their speech. Please be prepared to report to the full senate at next month's meeting."

The chairman went around the conference table and had each of us give our positions on the issue. Most were angry. They said it was hard to believe students would take our embassy in Iran, hold Americans hostage, come to this country, study at one of our universities, often live on student aid, and speak ill of this country.

When it was my turn to speak, no one made eye contact. "I find it hard to believe we are even discussing this," was my introduction. "Isn't this America? We are supposed to believe in free speech! I didn't come to the flagship University of Tennessee to watch free speech be denied to any of its students. Where is your moral outrage?"

All had quieted and were listening, but still no one made eye contact with me. I started looking around really for the first time. We were in a room with wall paneling the 1970s would have rejected. The male members of this committee all had the exact same haircut: short and parted to the side. Mine covered my ears and grew past the collar. They were all shaven, while I was rocking my first mustache that I would keep for the rest of my life. The guys wore Madras shirts and khakis with Docksiders. This was the unofficial uniform of Greek men of the 1980s. The women were not quite as uniformly dressed. Some wore shirts and slacks, and some wore sweaters; one was in a dress. I was in a cheap pair of jeans and a shirt, both purchased at the big-boy department at J.C. Penney's.

Committee chair Steve broke the silence. He asked if anyone else wanted to address the issue. All the other committee members were looking at their shoes. He called for a vote. We voted to recommend the first amendment be respected.

"When the SGA president asks for our recommendation then I will yield the floor to you. You will have two minutes to explain our stance. Call this our position, not yours. Understood?"

I made the same argument before the Student Senate that I had made to the committee. As I was concluding, I saw that the president didn't look very happy with me. When I finished, he told me they had done a poll of the student body, and 72 percent of them said they wanted the Iranian student protesters silenced. Didn't they have a duty to serve the will of the students? I had not made the argument he wanted, so now he needed to draw blood.

"I agree that the senate should heed the will of the people except when the issue of rights is concerned. At such times, leadership is required." I reminded this august body that if the will of the people were law, then black people in Montgomery would still sit in the back of the bus. Only whites would eat at food counters or get service in public businesses. "America is the crucible in which the medicine of freedom was ground, and without rights-minded servants of the people like our president, rights would cease to be the protection which we are guaranteed by God and the constitution. We must allow Iranians to speak freely or stop being Americans."

The president scowled at me as I took my seat. He thanked the committee for its report and asked for questions or comments. Seeing none, he called the question. Iranian students won. Word spread that I had stood up when needed, and I was elected to the Student Senate. The way the organization was structured, it was the vice president who had the most authority. She or he ran the committee system, which essentially was the same as the U.S. president's cabinet. After my year on the senate, I teamed up with another senator named Cal Kaiser, and we formed a student party to seek the elected positions of the student government. Cal was a West Tennessean with old family money and TV-personality good looks. I was the geeky sidekick. He financed the party along with the fees we charged the candidates, and I created the platform. We were the Purpose Party; during the campaign, Cal's purpose was to chase sorority girls, and I was the one campaigning early in the morning around campus. There were three parties running, and the other candidates were better looking and better known. It was in the campus debates I began to shine. We were asked a question by a reporter about how to deal with an internal student-government issue. The other candidates didn't know the issue and gave non-answers. When I answered, I explained the problem, gave my solution and ultimately was elected. Cal was not, but most of our party was. So there was a president from another party, named Fred Adkins. One-third of the elected seats were claimed by his party, and two-thirds were claimed by mine. I was a vice president with a majority, and if I could keep them happy, I would run the student government.

Deep into my term, an issue was brought to my attention by the research committee chairman, Robert Sexton. Knoxville had been selected as the host city of the 1982 World's Fair, and a neighborhood adjacent to the university called Fort Sanders was possibly going to be negatively affected by the fair. The neighborhood was a beautiful area, populated by historic homes and low-rent apartments. It was the site of a Civil War fort and contained a diverse group of residents including many UT students. Bob told me that residents throughout the area were being told that they would be evicted before the fair opening so that apartments could be rented at exorbitant prices to tourists visiting the fair. We met with his committee and decided to get the whole group to fan out across the neighborhood and survey the tenants to learn what they'd been told. Then we would make a list of landlords planning to evict and work to stop them.

We compiled a list of landlords who were threatening eviction. There were about 16 in all. I wrote each of them a letter, told them what their residents had told us and gave them a 10-day time to assure me this would not occur, or I would hold a press conference and release their names and contact information. Six responded, most admitting they had considered it but changed their minds. After the 10-day period, it was press-conference time. Ten names remained.

The morning of the conference, I was awakened by a phone call from Chancellor of UTK John Rogers. Dr. Rogers was a very kind, forward-thinking man, and I enjoyed our talks, but he never called me, especially in my room in the morning, so I jumped to the phone.

"Walt, I understand you have a big day ahead of you."

"You've heard about the press conference?"

"Heard about it? My phone has been practically dancing off my desk the last couple of days!"

"I'm sure it has. Who called? About what?"

"Landlords in Fort Sanders, Walt. It seems some young upstart is trying to interfere with their 'God-given rights as free Americans to evict their tenants and rent to fair visitors.'"

"Yes, sir, I guess I am."

"Walt, I have three questions."

"Yes, sir?"

"Why are you doing this?"

"Sir, university students deserve to be treated just like any other tenants. They sign six-month, yearlong or longer leases, give these landlords a living, and now just because a fair is coming to town, they are planning on putting students out on the streets, so they increase their profit? That hardly seems fair. Some of the students told us they don't have cars, and if they have to move too far away from school, they will have to go home."

"What will you do at the conference?"

"I'll explain to the press why we did the survey and announce those who didn't respond that they wouldn't evict and give out all their contact information. I will later provide this information to the City Council and see if there is anything they can do."

"Why didn't I first hear about this from you? I'm proud of what you're doing, and I would have liked to have backed you up from the start."

"Well, I thought if I kept you out of the loop, their anger would not be aimed at you."

"Walt, you should let me decide whom I anger. It just so happens, I think you're doing the right thing here, and I would've supported you if you had come to me. As a matter of fact, I'm going to back you anyway. Some of the landlords are threatening to sue you, so I told them if they did, since you are doing this as student vice president and with my full support, you will be represented by university counsel."

I thanked Dr. Rogers and held the press conference. The local media showed up in force because it was a story about the fair. It was later picked up by the "Today" show, and there was an article in the Wall Street Journal. The City Council passed an ordinance to help, but landlords have better lawyers. Eventually, the apartments where tenants were evicted attracted very few tourists due to the negative publicity, and most students stayed in their homes and had every chance to stay in school. No landlords attended, but in the back of the room sat a gray-haired man smiling through the conference. The media asked if he had any comments. He said I had said everything well. They asked, so he assured them I had full university support. Then Dr. Rogers draped his arm over my shoulder and invited this troublemaker to lunch.

In the spring, campaign time rolled around. Freddie wasn't seeking reelection, and a member of my party wanted to team up with me and run as my vice president. Lance Miller was a commuter senator who had worked tirelessly to improve commuter parking and campus security. We had become friends; he worked on many projects, including the Fort Sanders survey, and I thought he would make a great vice president. We threw our hats into the ring and formed a new party with the same name.

Lance and I had various similarities and differences. We were both hard workers. We both believed being elected meant that we were volunteering to work as servants for the public. We were both non-fraternity, geeky guys who could fit our girlfriends we had dated in our lives in the front seat of our cars.

The campaign was like most with lots of competition and not a lot of substance. I had a hard time pulling away from my duties and campaigning until I got a wakeup call from my former running mate's fraternity brother, Billy Carlisle. Billy was a tall, lean, future recipient of his daddy's money. He walked into my office one day in his frat-boy uniform of blue button-down shirt and tan khakis and his sockless shoes to tell me he would not be supporting me for president. "Why not?" I asked more out of courtesy than concern.

"During your term as vice president," he answered, "you've become well known and popular. Supporting you would be supporting the status quo. If I supported your opponent, and if I helped him win, that would look impressive on my resumé, don't you think?"

"Did you really come in here to announce to me that you're going to beat me?" I suspected he wanted me to make a counteroffer; maybe I could make him a campaign manager or adviser, but I had a team in place. My team supported my party because we shared common beliefs, not because campaigning for me would bolster their resumés. Billy then told me I hadn't really started campaigning, and everybody knew I was going to try to coast into the presidency on my laurels. He told me not to fear, he was sure I would pull the campaign out of the fire at the last second, and he would come by and congratulate me. "That's not necessary," I assured him. "I will be surrounded on election night with winners." I then walked his arrogant ass out of my office.

The first debate of the campaign took place in my former dorm. Hess Hall was a freshman dorm, and the fifth-largest dorm in the United States.

I served as its student senator; we were elected by geographic areas, and I became vice president there. I moved out as vice president, but because of my age and class status, no one was offended. My opponent, Tom Blank, was a fraternity man from one of the biggest and wealthiest frats on campus. He was from Pulaski, Tenn., the historic birthplace of the KKK. Hess Hall was big, noisy, diversely beautiful and not a stronghold for Mr. Blank.

During the debate, Mr. Blank was asked a question about his thoughts on my efforts to protect student apartments in Fort Sanders. Tommy explained to the audience that his best estimates showed that only about 300 people were affected by our survey and press conference. He explained, in an unnaturally deep voice used to compensate for his short stature and lack of integrity, that because only 300 people were affected, I had squandered the precious resources of the student government on an insignificantly small number of people. Then I got to respond.

"I was presented with a problem by the Research Committee. Students in the Fort were reporting that their landlords were going to evict them and rent their apartments to fair visitors. I heard from them personally that this eviction would cause many students to have to stop attending the university and would have a deeply negative impact on their futures. I believed then and I believe now that the student government should assist these students in any way possible. Mr. Blank seems to suggest that the SGA should only intervene in matters that affect a majority of our campus, but I believe we should intervene even if only one student is affected. It is, after all, a student government and to fail one student is to fail them all!"

The audience erupted, the reporters awoke, and I realized I had finally entered the campaign. The second debate was held at Presidential Courtyard. It was not a Walt-friendly area because the dorms surrounding the courtyard were mainly occupied by fraternity and sorority members who might not want a non-Greek president. I had gone to many of the Greek houses and rooms and talked of my goals as president; therefore, I had no intention of writing off their votes. When the debate started, I noticed I was getting eye contact and a chance. It was a crowd I could possibly win.

One of the questions I received was, "If the vice president of the opposition party was elected, and if you were elected, could you work cooperatively with him?"

I reminded them that the very scenario the questioner was posing was the situation during my vice presidency. I told them that there was friction at first, but we had learned to listen to each other and respect each other as the terms wore on. I would cooperate with whomever the students selected as vice president. With that, I added, "Lance came to me and asked that we run as a team. I said yes because I believed he would be an excellent vice president. His work in the senate has proven his wisdom, his determination and his interest in serving his constituents. As a matter of fact, he and I selected the whole party because these are all people we believe have the best interests of the student body at heart. If you wonder who will work best, then I ask you to elect all our party or elect my opponent. I want to serve with the best or not serve at all." My party erupted in applause! The opposition party split, and some of them applauded my speech. It gave our party a sense of unity that would survive past the election.

The last debate was in the courtyard on the eastern part of the campus. I lived in a dormitory near that courtyard. I was favored here. At the end of the debate, we were to give a closing statement. Tom went first and repeated his claim that I had squandered SGA time and resources helping only 300 students. He then told a long, winding story about ants working in an ant colony, and it made no sense whatsoever. I saw members of his own party looking at the ground, shaking their heads because they knew he failed them. When he finished he turned and walked to his seat, making certain not to make eye contact with me. I went to the microphone and said, "Like you, I have no idea what Tom's very long, pointless story about ants in an anthill was about, but I do know this." Every eye was on me, and everyone knew I was about to fatally draw Tom's blood. "If Tom were vice president of the anthill, all 300 of them would have been evicted!" The cheers from the crowd were deafening. The members of both parties were on their feet and cheering. The student reporters were cheering. I left the microphone, walked to Tom, and I whispered, "Touché, point, set, match." He still didn't make eye contact. He didn't need to. We both knew I had won, as did Lance and two-thirds of our party. Billy showed up to the victory party. I didn't let him in.

There were many successes during mine and Lance's administration.

Most notably we got an informal agreement on a 70:30 ratio of state funding for tuition where the state of Tennessee would use as its benchmark paying 70 percent of the cost of tuition and students would pay 30 percent. This formula allowed for tuition increases, but the student share of the increases would be contained, reasonable and somewhat predictable. Although this was never law, the agreement stayed in place around 20 years. We also worked as a part of a large coalition of people who successfully received funding for a new library.

Amid the successes, I had a few setbacks as well. In the late fall, my leg developed a sore on my lower shin, and my doctor recommended I stay out of my prosthesis until the leg healed. I was given use of a university wheelchair, and my friends agreed to help me get to classes. On Monday, Wednesday and Friday I had a class on the Hill, the highest place on campus, and then a Shakespeare class in the Humanities Building in the valley below the Hill. My friend Rebecca drew the short straw and helped me make this extraordinary journey. Rebecca was 5-foot-2 and not my first pick to get me safely up and down that hill. Yet she did it, day after day. She was behind me, so I couldn't see what she was doing, but she got me up that hill and back down again, and I lived to tell the tale.

In the Humanities Building, we met a challenge that even Rebecca couldn't overcome. There was no elevator, and my class was on the third floor. We finally decided there was only one solution: I would get out of the chair; Rebecca would pull the empty chair to the third floor; and I would crawl on my hands and knees up the stairs, reclaim the chair, and go to class.

One day, as I came within two steps of reaching the half-floor turn to continue to the second floor, I crawled up to a pair of dress pants and nice shoes in front of me. I looked up and Dr. John Rodgers, chancellor, was standing before me. "Either this is the oddest protest I have ever witnessed, or something is about to be explained to me that will leave me quite ashamed. Come sit by me, Walt, and tell me which one is true." He sat on the landing two steps ahead of me and I joined him. "Why are you crawling, footless up the stairs?"

I reminded him I do everything footless and being without my prosthetic just made it more obvious. He was in no mood. "Please tell me what you're doing."

I explained about my leg wound, my friend Rebecca, and the fact that there is no elevator in the building. He told me he could have arranged to have the class meet on the first floor. I told him there would be 31 people having to change their schedules, not counting the first-floor class being displaced, and I thought it better to bring me to the mountain. "You have my word that classes won't start next spring until an elevator is installed in this building, but that won't help you now, will it?"

I assured him this was not the first time I had crawled publicly, and it would probably not be my last. He asked if he could help me in any way. I thanked him and shook his hand, and as I reached the top floor, I looked back and saw he was watching to make sure I made it. That good man is in Heaven now, and I'm certain he did not take the elevator. He climbed step by step up the stairway he built by his good deeds while he was here. I often hope he and my grandfather met in Heaven. What a great meeting that would be between two of my greatest mentors.

# PART THREE
## Family

# CHAPTER TWENTY-ONE
## Church

I found a job in Knoxville, the same city in which I attended college. I taught English, and the first three levels of French when the need arose. The school was suburban, the students were mostly motivated and college oriented, and the parents were involved. I was too inexperienced to know I was teaching in Heaven, but I knew what I was doing was important, so I did it well.

In 1988, the school graduated one of my favorite classes. During that year, a group of students started meeting in my room before class and sometimes after school. We discussed politics, religion, philosophy, art, music, poetry, literature and our awkwardness at being human. Anita was not really a part of this group. While friends with each of them, she did not meet regularly with the rest of us. One day she came in while we were talking, and she asked me if I attended church. I explained that I grew up in a church, attended one in college and had not turned away but had not found one in Knoxville in which I was comfortable. Anita Schmid was the daughter of Dr. Rev. John Schmid, a local Presbyterian minister.

His church, Westminster, was known as a liberal, tolerant congregation. I had considered visiting but never had. Anita assured me that I would enjoy visiting Westminster. The people were great, and her dad was an extraordinary minister. A couple of other students chimed in that they attended the church and said it was one of the most important influences of their young lives. I promised that I would give it a try.

That next Sunday, I slipped into my blue blazer, blue button-down shirt, khaki pants and a tie, and I went to church. The congregation was full and friendly. There were several families with kids I had taught who attended, and we talked for a while. I enjoyed the sermon and had a brief conversation with Dr. Schmid after the service. He asked if I would mind if he visited me sometime soon. I gave him my phone number and said I wouldn't mind. As I got into my car to leave, I had no idea I had just changed the very direction of my life. When those forks in the road come upon you, you seldom see them for what they are, but had I known I was choosing a path, and if I could have seen where the path would lead, I would have taken it anyway, for better or worse indeed.

A few days later, I received a letter written by a man named Tony Cray. Tony was a Sunday school teacher at Westminster who taught a young-adult class. They were about to start a new study series, and Tony invited me to be a part of the class. I had never visited a church and received an invitation to attend a class before. I decided that Tony either really cared about his class, or the church was extremely welcoming. Either way, I was impressed enough to give the class a try.

I entered the class that next Sunday, met Tony and took a seat on the right side of the room. This was unlike me because the door was on the left, and normally I would sit near it, leaving me an escape. I allowed myself to be trapped.

Then She entered. She wore a pretty blue-green dress and was accompanied by a young man in a just-post-college suit. Her name was Heather, and She was as lovely as a flower. She had beautiful skin, a shy, sweet smile, and She had the bearing of a woman who had spent many hours in a church setting. Tony obviously noticed her, too. He directed an unusual number of questions to her during the class. Every time She attempted to answer, her boyfriend, Ronald, answered for her. At first, I thought I was imagining this trend, but every single time Tony asked

Heather a question, Ronald chimed in with an answer, looking proud of himself. Sometimes, Heather would follow up his comments with her own response, an act of defiance I admired. After the class, I introduced myself to Heather, and looking Her in the eye, I assured Her that if She were with me, I would listen intently for Her responses.

A few months passed, and I joined a group of people who were interested in joining the church. Heather was also in the group. We were taught in classes on the history of Presbyterianism and what it means to be a Presbyterian in today's world. Then I got a call from the Reverend Dr. John Schmid, who wanted to visit me. We agreed on a time after I could get home from work. He arrived right on time, and we sat across from each other in my very small living room in my modest basement apartment. He started by asking me several questions about where I was from, about my family, school experience, etc.

I told Dr. Schmid that I had grown up a member of a church and had loved it. I enjoyed the sense of community it offered and the friends I had made there. He asked if I would feel more comfortable in a Methodist church. I acknowledged there were differences, but I didn't think the differences were significant enough to keep me away.

Finally, when we boiled down to the basics, I told him that I didn't believe in a God of judgment. From the early church until today, the church seemed to place an enormous emphasis on God judging us and deciding whether we were worthy of His kingdom. I felt God was more like a loving parent who loves and guides His/Her children. Dr. Schmid read me many passages about God's love and loving nature. I told him I didn't believe in Hell or that anyone could be so bad that they would have to be cast away for eternity. Dr. Schmid handed me the Bible and said if I could find a passage that said you had to believe in Hell to get to Heaven, he would leave with me.

I couldn't of course. I liked him. More important, I began to trust him. He didn't seem to be trying to sell me something. He invited me to "go on a journey" with the congregation, to think, challenge and reflect. Joining the church was a commitment to try to understand what it meant to be a loved child of God. I joined Westminster early one beautiful Sunday morning, and I was pleased to see Heather was standing with me to join, too.

# CHAPTER TWENTY-TWO
## Joining

To join the church, we who wished to join had to appear before the church Session, which is the group of elders who along with God's guidance and the minister govern the church. We were asked a few questions that were intended to be routine but were actually complicated. "Did we accept Jesus Christ as the Son of God? Was He God in man form who had come to Earth to save us from our sins? Would we support the church financially and with our attendance and participation?" I had many opinions, long-winded answers and questions to toss back to them, but I decided this was no time for a discussion and obediently answered, "Yes." We were accepted, then we were stood before the congregation. I stood beside Heather trying not to look at her too much because I was joining the church for my own spiritual growth, and the congregation was asked if they would accept us as members and encourage us to become full, participating members of this church. They said, "Yes," and we took our seats.

Heather and I sat beside each other. Instead of focusing on the sermon, I found myself wondering why Ronald wasn't here to support Heather.

I was glad he wasn't there. When I glanced at her, she would return my gaze. I tried to stop being silly and pay attention. Impossible. She smelled too nice.

After the service, we were invited to lunch by the new members committee of the Session. I asked Heather if she'd like to ride with me to the restaurant. She said yes, and during the short ride, she explained that Ronald lived in Kingsport and only visited on occasion. "I would have thought that joining the church would be an important enough occasion for him to come to town."

"Are you sorry he isn't here?"

"Absolutely not," I assured her, as we entered the restaurant. The rest of the group sat at a large, crowded table, so Heather and I sat at a table near them. She told me she had grown up a member of the Baptist church. I asked her why she switched. She had come to the University of Tennessee as I had and stayed after, taking a job as a teacher. She had visited several churches, and Westminster seemed like the best fit to her. We talked throughout the meal. She was very good company, and I thought she'd make a good friend.

We joined the church in August and became telephone buddies after that. One day, she called me and said she had just had a terrible day. We discussed some discipline techniques that had worked for me, and she said she was going to lie down and sadly drop off to sleep. I then advised her that, "Just because you have a bad day at work doesn't mean you have to have a bad day in life."

"That's a great perspective!" she exclaimed. I told her there would be many terrible days in teaching and many great ones. If we let our lives depend on what others did, we'd never be happy. We continued to call for the next several weeks until December. The last day of the semester that year was on Dec. 17. I got the brilliant idea that Heather and I should go to dinner that night to celebrate. I wouldn't call it a date; I'd call it a celebration. That way she wouldn't start worrying about Ronald, who incidentally hadn't visited since we joined the church. I called her a few days in advance and asked if she would be available to celebrate the end of the semester with me on the evening of the 17th. She asked what the celebration would entail. I suggested dinner and a movie. She agreed and sounded excited. I got off the phone so my heartbeat could slow back down again.

She said she would meet me at my apartment since we were going out on my side of town. She arrived as I had just gotten home from a receiving of friends at a funeral parlor. An acquaintance of mine had passed away, and I had dropped by to pay my respects. I was still in my suit when I opened the door and invited her in. Her eyes were huge, and she shouted, "You're not wearing a suit, are you?" I assured her I wasn't. She came in and sat down while I changed. I resisted the temptation to come out in a robe, or to ask her to undress with me. I didn't think she would be amused, and I really liked Heather. I didn't want to run her off.

I changed and took her to dinner. We went to a restaurant selected for its proximity to the theater where the movie we chose was playing. Our dinner was pleasant; she felt obligated to discuss Ronald since she was, in her words, "cheating" on him by being out with me. She said this with a smile. I told her it wasn't cheating to celebrate together. That must have satisfied her because we stopped talking about him.

When we finished the meal, I paid the check and we stepped outside. The movie theater was a short walk across the parking lot from the restaurant. There was an unforeseen problem. During our meal, it had rained. The temperature was in the upper 20s, so the parking lot was covered with a thin layer of ice.

I turned to Heather and explained my predicament. "I don't have feet, and because of that, I wear prosthetic legs. I have entire legs, heels and ankles, but since there are no feet, I wear prosthetics that give me feet and a shell that goes up to just below my knees for balance. Because my "feet" don't move or react to sudden changes, I have great trouble walking on ice. Do you mind if I hold onto your shoulder and gently glide with you across the parking lot?"

She looked at me for a few moments before responding. I'm sure she was surprised that we had gotten this far in our friendship without me telling her the full extent of my physical differences. She turned to fully face me and asked, "You don't have feet?"

"No, I don't. Here, let me show you the prosthetic ..."

"Don't, please. I am going to trust you. You can hold onto my shoulder and we'll cross the parking lot. When we get to the other side, then please show them to me. If this is all a corny gag to get to put your arm around me, this will be our last 'celebration.' If you do have prosthetics, we'll go watch the movie, and I'll look forward to hearing all about them later."

I accepted her terms. Crossing the lot wasn't too precarious. During our crossing, I found myself praying God wouldn't give me feet now, turn me into a liar and cause me to lose this sweet woman. On the other side, she smiled and said, "OK, Bub. Show me your gams!" I lifted my pants legs to the knees, so she could see them. She glanced down, smiled, took my hand. We got popcorn for the movie.

I took her back to my place to get her car. I told her I had put up my first Christmas tree and invited her in to see it. Much to my surprise, she agreed. Inside, I took her coat and draped it over a chair. There was a closet right by the front door. I could tell she was wondering why I didn't put the coat in it. I confessed I was a terrible housekeeper, and if I opened the door, we might be killed by the avalanche. Fortunately, she laughed. We sat by the Christmas tree on the couch. The lights were all white, and they reflected in our glasses. She was wearing a reindeer sweater and jeans and looked warm and relaxed. We had a glass of eggnog and discussed Christmases past. She confessed that her mother was an alcoholic who was normally an intoxicated, bipolar mess during the holidays. She asked why, at 31, I had just put up my first tree. I made some terrible joke, and she responded that I could tell her. It was OK.

"When I was around 10 years old and my little brother was 6, our father told us one Saturday morning that we were going to take a walk on our farm and cut down a Christmas tree. We were excited to get a tree, so we bundled up and went outside to join Dad. It had snowed the night before. There was maybe an inch of accumulation and all was clean and fresh looking. Our family's farm was 50 acres that essentially blanketed over a ridge. One half was on the south side, one half on the north. "Now, you remember from our experience earlier, what do I have trouble doing?"

"You have trouble walking in snow and ice."

"Correct. My dad and brother had no such problem and quickly began to leave me behind. Because Dad raised cows on this land, including the occasional angry bull, we kids were not allowed to go into the pastureland unsupervised. I didn't know my way around. As Dad and little Frankie got farther and farther away, and as I ascended the hill, the house was harder and harder to see, so I became scared. I called out to Dad and Frankie, "Wait! Wait for me!' They kept going. I shouted, 'Dad, Frankie, wait! I can't keep up, and I'll get lost!'

"Dad shouted something to me, but I couldn't hear what he said. They were near the top of the hill in the tree line, and I knew I wouldn't be able to see them. I could possibly go back to the house, but I couldn't see it. There was no guarantee. I wanted to help get the tree. I decided my dad the Marine would appreciate my pushing ahead despite my uncertainty, so I pushed on, shouting for them to slow down all the time.

"As I came to the tree line, my dad and brother were not visible. I began to do the one thing my dad hated most. I started to cry. Dad soon came out of the woods, and he picked me up by the back of my belt and the back collar of my shirt. He carried me to where Frankie was. The entire time he carried me like a sack of potatoes, I kept shouting, 'I'm sorry, Dad! I didn't know where you were! I was just scared!'

Dad held me chest high at arms' length. "I shouted for you to wait, but you just had to have a little cry, didn't you? Do you know what I do to crybabies? I drop them." Dad opened both hands, and I fell to the ground face first. He picked me up the same way and dropped me a second time. I was strong enough to protect my face, but my hand, arm and knees were taking a beating. I stopped crying. On the third drop, I wanted to fall to show him I wouldn't break. I slowly stood up, knees and arms bleeding, and I looked in his face. He picked up his ax and chopped down a small cedar tree. He then pointed at it and told me to drag the tree down the hill to the house. He said I wouldn't be allowed to enter if I didn't have the tree with me. Then he and his junior began the easy walk home.

"I knew that if I stood there and thought about what had just happened, I would get colder and more scared, so I took the tree by the trunk and started pulling it downhill As I walked slowly toward a home I didn't want to enter, an anger began to swell up inside me. I could feel heat emanating from the wounds on my arm, hand and knees, and I imagined melting away all this slippery snow. I wanted to melt away my dad, too, and his trees, and stupid holidays that just got me in trouble. When I arrived at the house, my mom came running out to greet me. She looked at my arms and knees and started crying. She took the tree into the house and left it for everyone else to put up. She took me to the bathroom, washed my wounds and assured me my daddy loved me and was trying to teach me to be strong. That's when I broke her heart for the first time. I responded, "That's too bad. I hate him." I decided this year, I wanted to reclaim good things in my life. I put up a tree and celebrated with you, tonight."

Heather slid over by me on the couch and put her arm over my shoulder. She said, "With your dad and my mom, I guess we're a mess, huh? Maybe not, though. After all, we can still agree the tree is beautiful."

"Maybe we can agree that you are beautiful, too." I took a moment and really looked at her face. Heather had brown eyes that were sparkling with Christmas lights. She had those cute reindeer running around her midsection, brown shoulder-length hair and a kind, friendly smile. I was drawn in, closer and closer, our heads were tilted slightly to the right, and before I could logically talk myself out of doing it, I kissed her. Her lips were warm and sweet, and I could hardly be blamed for going in for a second.

It was time to slow things down a bit. After all, she was dating someone else; however, even I wasn't a dumb-enough jackass to bring him up at this time. We went to my CD player and saw my complete Indigo Girls collection. "Why do you have these?" she asked.

I told her my political leanings ran to the left, and I enjoyed their music and the intelligence of their lyrics. I don't know if it was my stories, my understanding of her past or the music that weaved a magic web around us, but we carelessly laughed, tickled each other and kissed until the wee hours of the morning. I was sad to see her go but confident she'd be back. We were both going to visit our parents, and she would see Ronald, but we would get back together when we returned.

I sat by a window in my apartment facing east and watched as the sun rose. I waited for him to fully awake, and then I spoke to him. "Guess what?" I asked.

"What?" he responded.

"I had a date last night with the woman I'll marry!" I nearly shouted!

"I can never leave you alone, can I?" We had a good laugh. The moon was visible but said nothing because she was there the whole time and said nothing.

142

CHAPTER TWENTY-THREE

# Heather

At the end of our "celebration" night, Heather and I agreed to call each other when we returned from our trips home. I got back late, and I wondered if she still wanted to see me. I was realistic; I knew she would spend time with Ronald over the holiday and with her parents, and she might be wondering if I fit into the picture at all. I knew I would have to work this intelligently or I might run her off. When I walked into my basement apartment, I saw the light on the answering machine blinking. I wondered if it might be she. I was renting the basement of a small house, and married friends of mine, Barry and Gail, were renting the upstairs. I was like the clingy teen who won't move out of his mom's basement. At least I paid a third of the rent and half the utilities, so we got along.

I hit the button; it was Heather. "I'm back in town. I've been thinking about you and would love to see you when you get in." I went to my kitchen to get a soda. Gail came down the stairs that joined my basement apartment to her upstairs apartment. She asked if I wanted to watch a movie with her and Barry. She sweetened the pot with the promise of sandwiches and popcorn, so I grabbed some sodas and upstairs we went!

While we were getting ready to start the movie, Gail asked if I had called Heather yet. I told her I had not but that she had left me a message earlier.

"What did she say?"

"She asked me to call when I got in."

"Why are you here? Go call her, silly!"

"Not yet."

"What are you doing"?

"I have a plan."

After the movie was over, I thanked Gail and Barry for the movie and snacks. I decided instead of calling Heather, I'd drop by to see her. On the way over, I wasn't sure if this strategy would work, but I didn't just want to chat on the phone. I knew Heather had enjoyed some Ronald time, and I needed to go big or go home.

I picked up a simple flower arrangement and knocked on her door a little after 9. She was very surprised to see me but invited me in. We sat on her couch and talked about our trips home. She said she had talked to Ronald about me. He knew we had been out together. I told her I wasn't trying to cause trouble; this was not true.

"I'm not trying to complicate your life. If I'm becoming a problem for you and Ronald, let me know. I will get out of the way."

"It's not that," she responded. "When I talk to you, I feel like you do more than listen. You mentally put yourself in my place. You meet me with empathy. You stand in my shoes. You understand my joy and pain because you feel it. Ronald acknowledges it. Then he shares his story, which may not be at all related to mine. You and I are connected. He and I know each other."

Then the phone rang. It was Ronald checking in. Heather put him on hold, and we walked outside. "You're not in the way," she said. "You've never been in the way."

"It's like we are two parts of the same person," Heather reassured me.

I gave her a kiss. "Go talk to Ronald. I'll be back when you're ready." She looked at me both smiling and with a tear in her eye. She was partially wrong about me. I wasn't sure exactly where she was now, and I was standing on a plateau all alone. When she went back in, looked back and smiled at me, she was reassuring me she could and would find me again. I would never again be left completely all alone.

# CHAPTER TWENTY-FOUR

# Birthday

Heather and I continued to see each other more and more frequently. She would still get a call from Ronald from time to time, but he didn't seem overly alarmed that she was pulling away. When she practically moved into my small basement apartment, she had a long talk with him, and the calls stopped.

We dated for a year and a half. It's the summer days I remember best, when she would show up in her khaki shorts, a T-shirt and Birkenstocks. She was completely irresistible. Our relationship was full of love, books, talking about issues, talking about family, talking about emerging from ugly childhoods, movies, food and love again. Her birthday was in November. It was our first birthday for her together as a couple. I planned to make it memorable. It was the day of the University of Tennessee versus Notre Dame football game. Heather had played in UT's Pride of the Southland Marching Band in college and loved to watch the games. We had agreed to meet at my place to watch the game, and I told her to bring something nice to change into, and I would take her out for a birthday dinner.

She arrived, and I had snacks for the game. We watched and reminisced about our college days. She seemed to be looking for something she didn't see. I made no excuses for not having a birthday cake or gifts.

After the game, we changed, and I told her I wanted to take her to Regas Restaurant. It was a wonderfully classy restaurant in downtown Knoxville that served the best steaks and red velvet cake in town. She was concerned about the cost, but I assured her it was going to be fine. We had to fight through game traffic to get there, and when we arrived, the lobby was packed. Heather looked very concerned, but she had no reason to be. After a brief wait, the manager walked over and said, "Mr. Nelson, it is so nice to have you dining with us. Won't you follow me?" Heather looked shocked as we followed him to a small table for two in the main dining area. A waitress came, welcomed us and took our order. When I saw the waitress coming back our way, I couldn't help but smile. She was carrying a long box tied with a ribbon, and she placed it in front of Heather.

"These have been sent to you, I believe, ma'am."

"What could this be?" Heather asked with a smile.

"Open it and see!" I urged her.

She did and took out a dozen red roses. Everyone in the room was watching. After she had been holding the flowers for a moment, she noticed a small square velvet box. I stood, and then I knelt before her. I was a knight in khakis, tie and blue blazer, bowing before my queen. "Will you be my wife?" I asked.

"Yes!" she exclaimed. She leaned over and kissed me as the room erupted in applause.

"Happy birthday," I added.

"The best," she assured me.

We went back to my place where I called her dad and asked for his daughter's hand in marriage. He seemed to be genuinely happy for us, even though I was a poor boy from the wrong side of the tracks. I had already told my parents I was going to propose, so their response was, "Well good. Uh huh." I'm sure when they hung up, the only act of celebration was my dad turning the TV volume back up. That's OK. Heather and I had a celebration of our own.

# CHAPTER TWENTY-FIVE
## The Revelation

Heather and I married in the church where we'd met. Dr. Schmid officiated, although he led to the first big fight Heather and I had had. During our couple's session with the minister prior to the wedding, Dr. Schmid asked if it was ever OK to lie to your partner. Heather, being the sweet angel, said, "NO!"

I rolled my eyes, and Dr. Schmid caught me. "That disturbs me, Walt. You don't agree."

"Of course not. I live on a little place called Earth and from time to time, a little lie is necessary."

"Really?" he asked, one eyebrow raised. "Give us an example of when it's necessary."

"OK. Heather comes home with a new haircut. She asks if I like it, and I think her stylist must be the 'Texas Chainsaw' murderer. Do I say that? No, I tell her she is always beautiful to me, and welcome her home with a kiss."

"Well, you squeezed past that one," he chuckled, but she wasn't so easily convinced.

A friend of mine from college, Daniel Gray, was my best man. He had everything organized the day of the ceremony. Neither of us believed in leaving things to chance, so Daniel had people posted around the perimeter to ensure that no one got out of hand and that no mischief was afoot. Everything went off smoothly, the reception afterward was lovely, and our marriage was off to a great start.

Apparently, my brother Frankie decided getting married wasn't too bad of an idea because he proposed to his girlfriend, Christie, about five years later. The whole family loved Christie immediately. She was friendly, helpful and supportive. When we were all visiting my parents, Heather would stay near me regardless of what was going on. Christie was more of a helper; she would be in the kitchen helping Mom or Beth prepare meals, wash dishes, etc.

The most important thing she did was love my brother. He went through a stage where he was a bit dangerously unpredictable. Christie put a stop to all that. She would not stand around and watch him self-destruct no matter how much she loved him. To his credit, he understood this and picked her over a risky lifestyle.

The two never had children, but when Heather and I had our two, Ciara and Aidan, Christie showered them with gifts and hugs. She clearly delighted in talking with them; that made her family to me.

One month before Frankie's wedding, my sister, Beth, and my mom planned a shower for the couple. It was scheduled for a Saturday afternoon at my parents' church. Heather and I went to Clarksville for the shower and tried to help as Mom swirled happily trying to get everything ready for the party. When she had gone all morning without hearing from Beth, she knew she needed to call. Beth worked several jobs to make ends meet and was not known for punctuality. When Mom called, sure enough, Beth was still asleep. "You need to hurry!" she urged her. "Don't go back to sleep, or you'll miss the whole thing." It was a rainy day. Mom worried about Beth. She worried about the food. She worried no one would come because of the weather. Mom worried. She had every right to worry. Beth drove onto Interstate 40 and the rain became harder and harder. As she was nearing an exit, she pulled between two speeding semis. The turbulence caused by the speeding trucks, and my speeding sister, and the blinding rain caused her to lose control of her car. Beth's car swerved off the interstate, jumped a ditch, and wrapped around a tree. The force of the flying car, the exploding airbag, and the impact of the car hitting the tree combined, and my sister's neck was broken. She did not survive the crash. When I learned she had died, I left the house, walked around behind my dad's truck and released a garbled scream and shout the likes of which I have never heard before or since. It was as if hearing she had died put a poison in me I had no choice but to purge. I was hoping no one would come to me. I had to suffer alone before I could mourn with them. She was a year and two months older than I, but I felt more like her twin. We understood each other. We supported each other. We had lived through the same history together. Beth was the glue that held us together as a family, and I wondered if we would stick together without her. We would, but not indefinitely.

Frankie and Christie never had their shower. During a family meeting, Frankie graciously offered to postpone their wedding to give everyone some grieving time. Only I spoke up. I told him that I believed this family could use some happiness. I thought they should marry as scheduled. There was no dissenting vote, and the decision was made.

The night before Frankie's wedding, the wedding party met at the church for a rehearsal and a rehearsal dinner. The groomsmen and bridesmaids acted as foolishly as possible to ensure there was not too much solemnity to the proceedings. We made fart noises as we marched up the aisle, we burst into song at the wrong times, we snored through the practice vows and we did all we could to not notice the candle that would be lit in remembrance of Beth.

After we ran through the practice ceremony a couple of times, the minister surrendered, and we all went to the church basement for a potluck dinner. We ate too much food, toasts were made and everyone seemed truly happy for the couple. When I heard the last toast and had offered my own, I decided to step outside for a breath of fresh air. I looked around outside and saw my dad standing by himself staring off in the distance. I walked up beside him and recognized that far-off existential gaze on Dad's face that all Nelsons have when we are thinking thoughts that transport them far away. I broke the silence. "Penny for your thoughts?"

"You're overpaying," he joked.

"Without question, but it's my money to squander."

He paused some more, then spoke. "It has dawned on me that I only had one child who loved me, and now she's dead." I had never seen the old man so sad and vulnerable. I didn't want to respond with something that would hurt him. Unlike my dad, I took no pleasure in causing pain.

I also felt I shouldn't walk away from a teachable moment, so for good or ill I said, "Permission to speak candidly, sir?" He turned toward me and looked at me for a moment, then nodded. Like a tired Napoleon standing on the hills overlooking Waterloo, flatulent, exhausted and defeated at the end of the wars he caused, my dad nodded his consent. "The children who don't love you are still here. Perhaps there's time."

Dad gave no response. I was expecting him to attempt to strike me, but his arms never moved. He turned back to look at the point at which he was staring when I came out and allowed his body language to dismiss me. For a moment, I substituted the fear he always made me feel with a desire to reach out to him. I wanted to find common ground in our grief to right past wrongs and build a brighter future. Yet, as was true of all his life experiences, all Beth's death had taught Dad was that only his grief mattered. The bridge between us was his to build. I had never hurt him, and he turned away from me. After a lifetime of hurting me, beating me, choking me, humiliating me and being disappointed in me, he turned away. I was not angry with him. I did not hate him. I walked back into the basement and simply didn't give a damn.

# CHAPTER TWENTY-SIX

# The Request

It was midweek, and Frankie was normally a weekend caller, if at all. Mom had been hospitalized a week ago. She had survived but wasn't sure she would survive the treatment she had received. No matter the progress her body was making, she kept saying the treatment had "broken" something inside her. I've never fought cancer, so I can't say I understood what she meant, but no amount of good news from doctors could persuade her she was fine.

She had gone to see her doctor a week earlier, complaining that she felt tired. He ran a few tests and found she was severely dehydrated, so he put her in the hospital. When she was rehydrated, he found she had pneumonia and was suffering from pain from her chemo and radiation treatments. She was in constant pain, and now Frankie was calling.

"Walt, I hate to say it this way, but if you want to say goodbye to Mom, you had better come to Clarksville.' I could tell by the urgency in his voice he was sincere. I pulled Heather and the kids together and explained that

Grandma wasn't doing well and we were going to Clarksville tomorrow to let her know we loved her and were thinking about her.

We arrived midafternoon and had a little trouble finding the place. Clarksville had recently closed the hospital in which I had been born to make way for a new one. They failed to tell me they rebuilt on another site. The new hospital was bigger and more beautiful than the old one, but that didn't make me any happier to be there. I was aware I might be saying goodbye to my mother that day, and I wanted to do it just right. Mom was in a less restricted Intensive Care Unit. She could be visited, but only by one person at a time. I took the first turn. I said, "HI!" as I entered the room. I assumed I would surprise her since I hadn't told her I was coming. She didn't seem surprised at all. She motioned for me to sit beside her, and I did.

She looked very tired. "Are you staying at the house?"

"No, Mom. We just came in for the day."

"I'm glad you did. Are Heather and the kids with you?"

"Yes, but they will only allow us to come back one at a time."

"I know. They are afraid I'll enjoy myself."

"I'm sure that's it." She almost smiled. "Are you still in lots of pain?"

"Yes, and it's getting worse not better."

"The doctor says your numbers are improving and he's hopeful."

"The only number that is improving is the amount I owe him."

"Then quit being stubborn and get better so you can go home."

She smiled and reached up and touched my face. "Walt, you know I'm not going home. That's why you're here today. To say goodbye."

"Mom, I'm not here to ..."

"You don't want to say goodbye, but that's why you're here. I don't want to say goodbye either. We both know it isn't goodbye. I will always watch over you. I'm proud of you, my sweet boy."

"I'm proud of you, too. You gave me something most moms can't give their kids."

"I'm too sick for riddles. What did I give you?"

"It's more what you did for me. You gave birth to me twice. You brought me into the world like most moms do, and when I was ready for school, you fought for my right to receive a regular education instead of a special education. You'll remember that special ed was a class that taught kids how to fold boxes all day and placed students in low-paying, terrible jobs. By fighting to get me a regular education in an age where that wasn't required, you gave me life, and then you gave me the possibility of a life. I graduated from high school with a regular ed diploma, and I graduated from college with high honors. I married Heather and had two beautiful kids. I got a master's degree and worked as a teacher, and as the president of the teachers' association, all because you stood up for me with that principal at my elementary school as I began school. Your act of courage made my whole life possible. I love you, Mom. I owe you everything, and you can't go anywhere until you know that."

"Walt, there is something I need to ask of you." I knew immediately what it was. She has been asking for this for a long time.

"Now, Mom, you ..."

"Hush. You gave your speech. It's my turn. You know your father's health is worse than mine even though he's not in the hospital yet. His macular degeneration has left him unable to see anything but light and some color. His Parkinson's is worsening despite his medication, and the accompanying dementia has him always confused. It's time, son. It's time for you to make up with him. Don't send him to his grave with this burden."

"Describe for me what burden I'm leaving him with."

"You know what I'm talking about. You two have never gotten along. Let him know you love him, too. When I go, he will feel alone. Please don't let him."

"Let me be clear. You want me to talk with the man who has beaten me, locked me away, humiliated me and told me how disappointed he is with me and tell him I love and forgive him?"

"Yes. Be the bigger man. Tell him you love and forgive him."

"Mom, never in my life has he ever expressed remorse for how he has treated me. He has been either ashamed of me, mad at me or disappointed in me my whole life. What should I say? I'm sorry I wasn't good enough? Sorry I wasn't man enough? Sorry if my lack of hands and feet seemed weak to him? Should I apologize for being me? I'm not ashamed of me! My physical differences shouldn't have given him permission to abuse me! Do you even accept that he abused me? If he ever apologizes to me, I will be as gracious as I can and try to forgive. But I am not initiating the dialogue. He doesn't deserve it, and I don't owe it to him."

"That is my dying request. Do what you will. Send Heather in next, then the kids."

"I came here to honor you. You gave me two lives. Don't forget." With that I gave her the last kiss on the forehead I'd ever give her.

# CHAPTER TWENTY-SEVEN

# No Bridge

Dad called me a few days later and told me he needed my help. I asked what he needed. He told me Mom's condition had worsened. She was in intolerable pain. A couple of hours earlier, she had summoned the medical team working on her. She told them she couldn't take it anymore. She wanted them to stop all treatment. She wanted only pain medication to help her fade away as painlessly as possible. "What do you want me to do?" I asked while crying.

"Talk her out of it, of course! You're the public speaker guy. Talk some sense into her." His voice was trembling. He, too, was ready to cry.

"Is she really in a lot of pain?"

"Yes."

"If left untreated, will she pass away?"

"Yes."

"Doesn't she have a Do Not Resuscitate order?"

"Yes, we both do."

"Then, Dad, I think we should respect her wishes."

"Come on! We can't just let her die!"

"You're right. Will you drop your DNR in the mail for me, so I can tear it up and ignore your wishes? She has always said she wanted to be able to make this decision. I love Mom and want her to live. Now, we have to love her more than ourselves and let her go." He openly began to cry. I was crying, too. He acknowledged that I was right, and he hung up. Four hours later, Mom felt pain no more.

Frankie and I talked after Mom's funeral. Dad had started having at-home nurses before Mom died. Frankie found out how much they cost and realized this wasn't an arrangement that could be sustained long. Since Frankie lived in Clarksville, he agreed to be the one to find a retirement home for Dad. After a two-month search, he found a home that would accept VA payments, and the problem was solved. Dad wasn't very enthusiastic about moving into a retirement home, but he suspected at least one nurse was stealing from him, and for some reason, before he died, he wanted to sell off all he had. He accepted the living arrangement Frankie had set up with the understanding that Frankie would sell everything Dad owned.

This made me a little sad. Mom and Dad had the house I grew up in built when I was 3. I lived there until I moved out for college. Whenever I talked about "going home" I meant to my parents' house on Antioch Creek Road. On a few hills north of that paved country road was the property my first ancestors on my maternal grandfather's side of the family owned. The property was essentially on three hills; my Mom was born on the hill on the left, grew up on the hill on the right and lived with her own family on the hill in the center. I guess with Mom gone, Dad didn't want the land in the family anymore. Grandpa Walt's family had owned it only since the 1840s; Dad was no longer tied down by the family, so he rid himself of the burden of the land.

Frankie hired an auction group to come in to price everything and do the sale. He called me and gave me a few days to come to Clarksville to get any pieces of furniture I wanted. I needed a truck and a good friend to help me accomplish this, so I called on my Westminster friend Tony Cray and asked if he would go with me. When we arrived in Clarksville, we had already agreed to go see my Dad in the "home" before we went through town to where my parents had lived. We asked a receptionist where we could find him and walked down the hallway on the right. As we passed a nurses' station, one of the nurses made eye contact with me and giggled, "Oh, Lord, there's another one."

"I take it you know my dad and brother?"

"Yes, and you all look just alike!" All the nurses were smiling.

"And none of us are likable."

"Your daddy is down the hall on the left," she said, wanting free of me.

"Thank you." We proceeded down the hallway and walked into my dad's room. He was lying on his bed and looked barely awake. "Hi, Dad," I said as he sat up. "You remember my friend Tony?"

"Sure. Have a seat." We did so, and Tony reminded my dad of the few times they had met. I'm not sure if he remembered, but he was being very pleasant anyway. He told us about his new living conditions. The staff was OK. The food was edible. He was always cold. The room was comfortable. The only thing he hated was the showers. To shower, he said, he walked into the shower area and removed his towel, he was sprayed with water and given some body wash to use, and then he was rinsed off. He said the process made him feel like a bull being readied for sale. I told him I would talk with the nurse about it but wouldn't promise a change. That seemed to satisfy him.

He talked with Tony a few moments, and then I asked him if he knew me. He explained that he had macular degeneration and couldn't see well. He also knew he had Parkinson's and couldn't remember as well as he used to. I asked if he remembered having children. "Yes, we had three. The first was a girl. She had real pretty hair and was a great cook. Too bad really because all that cooking made her fat later in life, and she wasn't as pretty as she could have been." I'd heard him say this before, sometimes to Beth, and it always was untrue and insensitive. "My second kid was a boy. I was going to name him after me, but he turned out to be crippled."

Tony interrupted and asked why he couldn't name a child with a disability after him. Dad answered that: "A crippled boy could never quite be a man, could he?" Tony looked at me to communicate he was sorry he had asked. I was used to this. It wasn't new to me. Dad then said he had another boy child. That kid had been taking care of him since his wife died. He sold the property and helped him get the room in which he was now residing. That boy's name was his: Frank.

"Dad, this is Walt, the second child. Do you remember that Mom bought a van shortly before she went to the hospital?"

"Yes, I do. What about it?"

"I wondered, since you are selling off everything, if you'd be interested in selling the van to me. Ciara will turn 16 soon, and I'd like to give her the van to drive. I'll pay a reasonable price. What do you think?"

He didn't need to think. I'm pretty sure that as soon as he heard my name, he made up his mind. "I don't want to sell it," he answered.

"Mind if I ask what you'll do with it?" I knew the answer. He would give it to Frankie.

"Sometimes, I might want to get out of here and go for a ride. I'm keeping it, so I can go when I want."

I was angry at his refusal, so I asked a couple of questions. "Dad, what color is my T-shirt?"

"I don't know," he answered. "I can't see that far."

"If you can't see across the room, how can you drive?"

"I can see if I want."

"OK. Dad, you worked at the same factory for 35 years, right?"

"Yes, I did."

"Can you tell me the route you took to get there?"

"I don't remember," he responded.

"Then how are you going to go for a drive now?"

"I don't know, but I don't want you to have the car."

"OK, Dad. Tony and I are going out to the house. We're meeting Frankie out there and picking up a couple of pieces of furniture."

"What are you getting?" he almost shouted.

"Does it really matter?"

"No, I guess not."

As Tony and I left the room, I turned back and asked one more time. "Do you remember who I am?"

"No, I just remember I don't like you very much."

"See, you still have some of your memory."

A few days later, Dad was moved down the hall to the hospice wing.

# EPILOGUE

As I pulled into the parking lot of the hospice, I still had no idea what to say to a dying father. Since I had disappointed him my whole life, this would be just another failure. I walked through the door praying for guidance, and a receptionist greeted me. I asked her my father's location, then asked if a chaplain were on duty. "Not on duty, but we have a chaplain who is about a 20-minute drive from here. I'll be glad to call him to come here to meet with you."

"Thanks for your kindness, but I'll be fine." I started out of the lobby.

"It wouldn't be any problem to call. He would be happy to help." For some reason, asking for a chaplain made me feel weak and silly. I assured her I was fine and turned left into the main hallway.

I had never been in a hospice before that day, and apparently, they could tell. I was met just before I arrived at my dad's room by a nurse. She was brunette, about my height, and gave off the feeling of strength. She put her hands on my shoulders and stopped me. "Are you Mr. Nelson's son?"

"Yes, I am."

"You look a lot like him. He couldn't deny you." She smiled. "Have you ever been to a hospice, sir?"

"No."

"We get a lot of military types in here because of Fort Campbell, so I tend to be blunt with visitors. Are you OK with that?"

"Yes, ma'am."

"People don't come in here to get better, sir. They come here to die." I appreciated the candor. "I need you to understand that the doctors have done all they can do, and he has been brought back here to prepare to die.

161

We give him a little medication via a dissolving strip to help him with the sore throat he gets from gasping so hard to breathe. He is also on pain medication because he is in considerable pain and doesn't deserve to die in agony. When you see him, you may be shocked. His back is arched, and he struggles to breathe. His pain meds have knocked him out. He won't be conscious. Say whatever is in your heart. This may be the last time to say it. He cannot respond. Can he hear you? No one really knows. No one here is listening, so share with him whatever you want. I *am* going to call the chaplain. He is wonderful, and he'll be happy to speak with you. If he comes, and you don't want to talk with him, send him away. But I'm calling him, and he should be here in about 20 minutes." She walked me into the room, and I gasped. It was hard to look at my dad. He was covered with a hospital gown and a thin blanket. His back was arched, as the nurse said, and his labored breathing unnerved me. How was I ever to speak to him? "Just start talking. It will get easier."

I thanked her for her help and guidance. She smiled, and before she closed the door, she explained the nurses would come turn my dad in a few minutes. She smiled and closed the door, leaving me with the gasping twisting shell that was my father.

The nurses did come and turn him. He stopped breathing altogether, cried out in a single burst. They put him on his back with his head draped over the front end of the bed. The mouth was open, and his heavy breathing resumed quickly. Even now, I hate to hear the effect of pain. Even now.

I tried to talk to him. What do I say to this man? Words seldom fail me; today they couldn't find me. I decided to repeat his name and see if that helped. Frank Nelson, Frank Nelson. It was silly and contrived. We were never able to talk on normal days. I don't know why I thought today would be different.

I was startled when the door opened suddenly. My dad's nurse looked around the door and announced the chaplain was here, and she let him in. She reminded me that I could ask him at any time to go and he would. In walked a man who was about my build who was around 6 feet, overweight, and was wearing khakis, a blazer and shirt and tie. His soft hands said he had never worked hard in his life, but he slowly burned through my skepticism. He asked about me. Job? Family? Interests? Then he said he felt tension in the room. He asked about my relationship with Dad. It was hard to answer. We could never talk openly about feelings in his house.

"Not to be cruel but your dad is literally on his deathbed, he's unconscious, and he is unable to respond. I think you are free to speak." I explained that Dad was violent. I explained he would get upset with me for no reason. I explained that I reminded Dad that he and Mom had a baby out of wedlock, so I was a symbol of God's judgment and shame. I told him Dad was even ashamed that I had written a children's book and tried to help people understand people with physical differences. All he had ever wanted out of me my whole life was for me to sit behind him out of sight and to keep my mouth shut, and here I was in his hospice room sitting beside him wanting to talk.

The chaplain told me his mother was a tough woman to love. She was very angry with him and would criticize him for everything he did. She shouted often, and he felt worthless. He went into the ministry because his belief in God taught him God loved him, he had worth, and he wanted to share that with everyone. I told him it was difficult to call for God's help when a violent father slept in the room beside yours.

"Difficult as it may be, the help is always there," he assured me. Then changing directions, he asked, "Why do you think he wanted you sitting silently behind him?"

I told him that Dad believed I was a symbol of his sin. He believed I was a broken shell of the man he thought himself to be. With no hands or feet, I would always be the sad opposite of the mighty warrior Marine sergeant. He thought me useless and believed my book and speeches merely broadcast my shame.

The chaplain sat quietly and considered this for a while. His ability to really listen and to weigh what I was saying convinced me that I was glad he had come.

After ruminating a while, the chaplain turned and responded, "When you were first introducing yourself, you told me you are married with two kids, you've worked as a teacher over 30 years, you wrote a children's book to help children better understand people with disabilities, and you give speeches for the same purpose. Does all that sound accurate?"

"Yes," I replied. "It's accurate."

"You sound like a pretty good man to me. Is it possible your dad just couldn't understand the man his son had become? Maybe he wasn't smart enough to be your dad."

I didn't want to answer that. It seemed too disrespectful to say that with his dying body right in front of me. "I don't think he ever got past his perception of what he wanted me to be and allowed himself to see what I was."

"Who made that mistake, you or him?"

"He did. He never really looked or listened. He silenced and ignored."

"That is a burden he will be buried with. Don't carry it with you."

I told him it was getting time for me to make the four-hour drive home. He asked if we could end this part of our time together in prayer. I told him we could, and we stood on opposite sides of my father's bed.

"If you got to decide where your father would go from here, Heaven or Hell, which would you pick?" I don't really believe in Hell and said so. "You Presbyterians mess up everything!" he chuckled. "Imagine both exist. Which would you choose?"

I told him all of us make mistakes. "My dad hurt me, but he is still my dad, and I'd want him to be forgiven and to rest in Heaven."

"I believe that your forgiveness frees you." He asked me to put my hand on my dad as he prayed. When he was finished, he gave me one more suggestion before I left. "Every time you wonder why your father didn't love you, or understand you, or even try, I want you to go hug one or both of your kids. Your way out of this sadness is through not making his mistake. Love the family you have and accept them for who they are."

That night, back home in my bed, I had a dream. In it I was sitting in my dad's recliner napping when I heard a sound outside. It sounded like a whimper or cry. I left the house and instinctively walked toward the barn that had been knocked down when I was a teenager. As I entered the barn, I heard sobs coming from the stall I was locked in so long ago. I opened the door and saw Dad sitting on the floor weeping. I pulled a short three-step ladder up to the door and turned to leave. He smiled this distant, eerie smile, one born of cessation of pain and not from happiness. "You can get out or stay. The rest is up to you." With the sad grimace on his face, he looked less like my dad and more like a clown in cobwebs. "Suit yourself," I said as I turned and walked back to the house.

CPSIA information can be obtained
at www.ICGtesting.com
Printed in the USA
BVHW031102150820
586517BV00001B/177